The humble
Spud

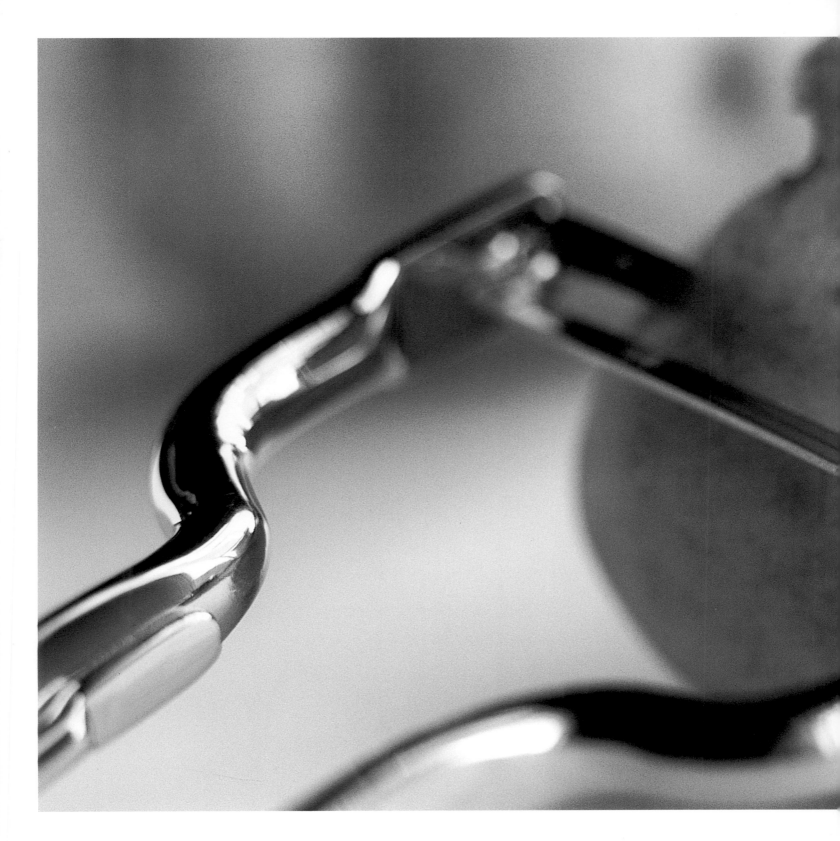

The Humble Spud

First published in 2000
by Hamlyn
an imprint of Octopus Publishing Group Limited
2–4 Heron Quays, London E14 4JP

ISBN 0 600 60173 0

Printed in China

Cover photography and Special photography: Philip Webb

All other photography: Octopus Publishing Group Ltd.

Home Economist: Dagmar Vesely

NOTES

1 The Department of Health advises that eggs should not be consumed raw. This book contains some dishes made with raw or lightly cooked eggs. It is prudent for more vulnerable people such as pregnant and nursing mothers, invalids, the elderly, babies and young children to avoid uncooked or lightly cooked dishes made with eggs.

2 Meat and poultry should be cooked thoroughly. To test if poultry is cooked, pierce the flesh through the thickest part with a skewer or fork – the juices should run clear, never pink or red. Keep refrigerated until ready for cooking.

3 This book includes dishes made with nuts and nut derivatives. It is advisable for those with known allergic reactions to nuts and nut derivatives and those who may be potentially vulnerable to these allergies, such as pregnant and nursing mothers, invalids, the elderly, babies, and children, to avoid dishes made with nuts and nut oils. It is also prudent to check the labels of preprepared ingredients for the possible inclusion of nut derivatives.

Contents

Introduction

The potato is a starchy edible tuber, which grows at the end of underground stems of the plant, *Solanum tuberosum*, a member of the nightshade family. Above ground, the plant has a stem and coarse, dark green leaves resembling those of the tomato. Its flowers range from white to purple. The tuber has external buds, or 'eyes', which can sprout into new plants.

Few foods have a more legendary past, natural diversity, fascination for scientists or greater potential to feed the world's population than the potato. It is the most familiar of all vegetables and one of the world's most important food crops. There are now more varieties than ever before, adapted for different climatic zones and grown in about 130 countries around the world. The potato can be cooked in more ways than any other vegetable. It is easy to grow, inexpensive to buy and extremely filling.

Potato history

Potatoes are native to South America. The first archaeological evidence dates back almost 6,000 years to areas in the Peruvian Andes where the potato plant is part of the native flora. It was cultivated in Peru and Bolivia and was a staple of the Inca diet. The influence of potatoes permeated the Incan culture and potato-shaped pottery complete with eyes is commonly found during excavations.

Incan units of time correlated to how long it took for a potato to cook to various different consistencies; potatoes were even used to divine the truth and predict the weather.

The potato was introduced to Europe from South America by Spanish explorers towards the end of the 16th century. Cultivation spread slowly from Spain to Italy, then Belgium, Germany and Switzerland. The crop was very slow to become established in England and Scotland, but was quite widely grown in Ireland by the beginning of the 17th century. It was early 18th-century Irish immigrants who took it to North America (where it is often called the 'Irish' potato, to distinguish it from the unrelated sweet potato), since it had failed to spread there directly from South America. Not until the 19th century did England and Scotland start to cultivate potatoes widely, followed on a large scale by France.

By the middle of the 19th century the potato had become the staple diet in Ireland and was also relied on as animal fodder. This dependence on potatoes led to intensive cultivation, which created ripe circumstances for the rapid spread of the fungal disease, blight. The potato blight struck Ireland three times in the 1840s, each time destroying most of the crop. The country's virtual monoculture meant there was nothing else for the people or their livestock to eat. Relief efforts were mounted, but were only partially effective and over a million people died. Between 1841 and 1851, Ireland's population fell from 8.2 million to 6.6 million through starvation, disease and emigration – to England and especially to the United States.

In the 20th century, the potato played a part during World War II – this time saving people from starvation. During the crisis in Britain, wheat imports from the USA and Canada were little more than a trickle and Britain's Ministry of Food used a cartoon character, Potato Pete, to encourage people to grow their own root vegetables in gardens and allotments.

The second half of the 20th century saw the introduction of and increasing reliance on convenience foods. There is now a worldwide market for an extensive range of dehydrated and frozen potato products, particularly the potato chip.

Today, scientists and agriculturists continue to study and develop new potato varieties. This results in making them higher yielding, more disease resistant and suited to a variety of climates worldwide. In developing countries, the production of potatoes is increasing faster than that of any other food crop.

Folklore

It is interesting to examine the different ways in which the potato has been regarded over time. While the Incas worshipped potato gods, the vegetable was often feared, reviled and shunned for the first few centuries following its arrival in Europe. At various times it was blamed for leprosy, scrofula and flatulence, and was also considered poisonous since it came from the same family as the deadly nightshade. It was also attributed with the ability to cure impotence, and had a reputation as an aphrodisiac in Shakespeare's England, according to *The Merry Wives of Windsor*.

Other sayings and superstitions relating to potatoes are of unknown origin. Laying a potato peeling at the door of a girl on May Day was said to show her that you disliked her, while a woman expecting a baby was not to eat potatoes, especially at night, or her baby would be born with a big head. A potato carried in the pocket was believed to cure rheumatism and eczema. Similarly, carrying a peeled potato in a pocket on the same side as a bad tooth would cure the tooth as soon as the potato fell apart. A person with a wart was advised to rub it with a cut potato, then bury the potato in the ground. As the potato rotted in the ground, the belief was that the wart would disappear.

Nutrition and health

With its high starch content, the potato was long regarded as being a 'fattening' food, but now a more complete understanding of nutrition has led to its rehabilitation. The addition of too much fat when cooking and serving potatoes is now recognized as the real culprit. By itself, the potato is in fact a near perfect food. It is 99.9% fat free yet rich in nutrients, containing a number of minerals and vitamins important for a healthy and nutritious diet.

According to food experts, a diet of potatoes and milk will supply all the nutrients the human body needs. Although potatoes are about 80% water, they provide a valuable source of easily digested starch, vitamin C, protein, potassium, iron, thiamine, niacin and dietary fibre, while containing almost no fat or cholesterol.

The vitamin C content is highest in freshly harvested potatoes – particularly 'new' ones – and steadily decreases thereafter. After three months' storage, the vitamin C content is less than half the original. Lengthy soaking of potatoes in cold water also diminishes their vitamin C content and should be avoided. Many of the vitamins and minerals found in potatoes are concentrated in or just under the skin and are therefore best retained by cooking potatoes in their skin or peeling them as lightly as possible. Potato skins are also high in fibre. Concerns over agricultural chemical residues in skins, which are not removed by scrubbing with water, can be addressed by eating organically grown potatoes.

Nutritional composition of a potato	
Water	81%
Starch	16%
Minerals and trace elements	1%
Vitamins	0.7%
Fibre	0.6%
Protein	0.35%
Sugar	0.27%
Fat	0.08%

Nutritional values per 100 g (3½ oz) raw potato	
Energy	79 kcal
Protein	2.1 g
Carbohydrate	17.2 g
Fat	0.2 g
Fibre	1.3 g
Sodium	trace

Introduction

Potato varieties

Potatoes vary considerably in size and may be round, oval, long and cylindrical or kidney shaped, depending on variety. They may be red - or brown - skinned or, more rarely, blue, black or purple. The flesh is mostly in the white to yellow colour range, although darker colours are possible.

Cataloguing the endless varieties of potatoes is difficult. Popular varieties change rapidly, coming into favour with growers because they keep well or are resistant to disease, only to be ousted by newer, even hardier varieties with higher yields.

Potatoes are often defined either as 'new' or 'old', or they are distinguished by texture as either floury (mealy) or waxy potatoes. Neither classification system, however, is without its anomalies.

The flavour of a potato depends on both its variety and its inherent texture. How and where it is grown and in what type of soil, and the weather in any one season all affect its flavour and quality. This explains why the same variety may taste better at some times than others.

'New' and 'old' varieties

In Britain, potatoes are divided into two main categories – early or new potatoes, and maincrop or old varieties.

Traditionally, British-grown new potatoes are varieties that are planted early in the year, grow fast, mature quickly and are available in late spring through to summer. They are eaten fresh, known for their delicate and sweet flavour and do not store well. With today's growing, storing and transporting techniques, modern 'new' potatoes are now grown all year and imported from various countries. Many, however, are actually maincrop potatoes, picked early when immature, and therefore disappointing in flavour. In general, new potatoes have a firm creamy waxy texture. Jersey Royals have a particularly fine flavour and have long been regarded as the king of true new potatoes.

Maincrop potatoes take longer to mature and are therefore larger. They are harvested during autumn when their sugar has converted to starch, and are stored and sold from harvest-time until the following spring, when the first new potatoes appear. In general, such potatoes tend to be floury in texture.

In the United States, potatoes tend to be classified more by shape, skin colour and use. Russets are good for a variety of uses but are best for baking. Rounded or long whites can be used for either boiling and baking, and small red and speciality gourmet potatoes are ideal for boiling. There, new potatoes are not a specific variety of potato, but any potatoes harvested early before the skins have set; they are best cooked by boiling or steaming.

Waxy versus floury potatoes

Potatoes with a firm, waxy texture have a high moisture content, low starch and thin skins. They do not break up during cooking and are therefore ideal for boiling and sautéing, for use in salads and for any dish where the potatoes need to remain intact after being sliced thinly and then baked, for example, a hotpot or gratin. Waxy potatoes become glutinous when overprocessed and are therefore not recommended for mashing and for purées. Floury-textured potatoes contain more starch and break up easily once cooked. They are generally best used for mashing, roasting and baking in their skins. Both waxy and floury types can be used to make chips (French fries).

However, there are no hard-and-fast rules. If you want baked potatoes and you have only waxy ones in the house, use them for baking. You will simply get a different-textured potato. In fact, the majority of potato varieties are neither especially floury nor especially waxy; most can be boiled, roasted, baked, chipped and so on. There are some all-purpose potatoes whose texture is described as firm and these can be used for almost anything – except perhaps

Introduction

potato salads. They don't disintegrate, but don't always have the best flavour.

So, although texture is sometimes a matter of choice and you will have to experiment to find your preferences, individual potato varieties do have their own characteristics. Undoubtedly, some varieties are better for baking than for boiling and vice versa – refer to packet directions or ask your supplier for advice.

Sweet potato

The sweet potato, *Ipomoea batatas*, is the starchy tuberous root of a tropical vine and is not related to the potato. However, it can be cooked in exactly the same way and is most successful baked and served with butter or mashed. In the USA sweet potatoes are sometimes wrongly referred to as 'yams', which are in fact another species of tuber.

Sweet potatoes are generally elongated and knobbly with pink skin and white, yellow or orange flesh. The yellowish flesh indicates the presence of carotene, a source of vitamin A. Choose small or medium-sized sweet potatoes, firm and well shaped; avoid any with cracks and damp patches. Differences in flavour between varieties result from the balance of sugar and starch. Sweet potatoes do not store well, but are cultivated all year round.

Popular potato varieties

FLOURY

Desirée
Golden Wonder
Green Mountain
Home Guard
Kennebec
Kerrs Pink
King Edward
Maris Piper
Norgold Russet
Pentland Crown
Pentland Dell
Pentland Squire
Pontiac
Romano
Russet Burbank
Sebago
Wilja

WAXY

Belle de Fontenay
Charlotte
Finnish Yellow Wax
Jersey Royal
Maris Bard
Maris Peer
Spunta
Pentland Javelin
Pink Fir Apple
Rocket
Roseval

Choosing and storing potatoes

When buying potatoes, choose ones that are well formed, with firm smooth skins. They should smell fresh. Avoid any with discoloration, cracks, bruises or soft spots. Don't buy or use potatoes with a greenish tinge to the skins – these have been badly stored, exposed to light and are unfit for eating.

Maincrop potatoes should be dry, with some earth on them, free of sprouts and with no green patches. New potatoes should be small, and you can judge their freshness by how easily the skin is scraped. Ragged skins that can be pulled off easily show the potatoes are very fresh. New potatoes sold ready washed should be taut and shiny. Buy new potatoes in small quantities only and use them quickly since they do not keep well and lose their flavour and texture after just a few days. Allow 175–250 g (6–8 oz) per person.

Storing

Potatoes should be kept in a cool, dark, well-ventilated place. In these conditions, maincrop potatoes can be safely stored for several months at a temperature of 7–10°C (45–50°F). Buy only a week's supply at a time if you must store them at higher temperatures since heat causes them to sprout and shrivel. Do not store potatoes in the refrigerator. Below about 5°C (40°F),

potato starch turns to sugar and results in the darkening of potatoes during cooking. Although unattractive, this is not harmful; the dark spots simply reveal the presence of a higher concentration of sugars. The process can be reversed by keeping the potatoes at room temperature, but still in the dark, for a couple of days.

Do not wash potatoes before storing since washing speeds decay. Brown paper bags are best for storing small quantities of potatoes. If you buy potatoes in a plastic bag, tear the bag so that they don't sweat. It is particularly important that the storage place is dark in order to prevent the development of solanine, which causes potatoes to go green. Although the green colouring (chlorophyll) itself is harmless, the green parts also contain high levels of poisonous alkaloids and should never be eaten. Make sure all the green parts of the potato are cut away; the rest will then be all right to eat. Never use potatoes where more than one tenth of the skin has turned green.

Potato sprouts also contain high levels of these poisonous alkaloids and should never be eaten. Similarly, once these sprouting parts are cut away, a sprouted potato is safe to eat, although it becomes softer and deteriorates in flavour and nutritional content.

Cooking Methods

Cooking methods

Potatoes can be cooked in a multitude of different ways and used whole, grated or cut into chunks. They form the basis of many traditional and regional dishes the world over, for example Swiss rösti, Irish colcannon, France's gratin dauphinoise and Niçoise salad, the tortilla of Spain and gnocchi from Italy. You can boil or steam them and serve them as they are, or mash them with additional ingredients for a jazzed-up version of traditional mash. Bake them in their skins, roast or sauté them, serve them as chips, barbecue or griddle them – the options for using and cooking potatoes are endless. Other than its obvious role as a vegetable in soups, main courses and side dishes, the potato can be successfully mixed with flour to make pastry, bread, dough and scones, and is used in sauces and some dessert recipes.

Interestingly, the widespread use and popularity of the potato accounts for the numerous culinary utensils that have been developed especially for it. Consider the potato peeler, the special knives available for cutting regular slices and potato straws, the chip cutter, the mashed potato scoop and the potato masher among others.

Remember that most of the nutrients and flavour in potatoes come from in or just under the skin, and are therefore lost when they are peeled. If you must peel potatoes, use a vegetable parer rather than a knife so as to pare the skin as thinly as possible.

Boiling and steaming

Potatoes cooked in their skins are better for you and tastier, too. Leaving potatoes unpeeled retains much of the nutrients and flavour found near the skin and affords the potato flesh some protection from the cooking water or steam, which dissolves the nutrients. Whether you keep the skins on after cooking is often a matter of personal choice.

Potatoes should spend as little time as possible in water because of its detrimental effect on nutrients. Cooking potatoes using the least amount necessary of boiling water, rather than bringing them to the boil from cold will reduce their contact time with water. However, opinions differ as to which of these methods you should use. Whether you prefer to cook them using cold water or add them to a saucepan of boiling water, use equally sized whole potatoes or cut the potatoes into even-sized pieces so that they will cook evenly. Cover the pan, again to reduce cooking time and therefore time spent in water, and cook the potatoes until tender – 10–15 minutes for new potatoes and about 20 minutes for maincrop ones, although this does depend on their size. Reduce the heat so as to cook the potatoes gently, since fast boiling causes them to bump against each other and break up. While this is not so important if you are intending to mash the potatoes, it is not desirable for gratins or potato salads.

When just tender, drain the potatoes thoroughly and return to the pan. Let them steam for a minute or so, or leave them in the pan covered with a clean tea towel to absorb the steam and produce dry rather than sodden potatoes.

If you are peeling potatoes, ideally do so just before cooking. However, if this is not feasible, place the peeled potatoes in a bowl of water to prevent them from drying out and, in the case of some varieties, from discolouring on exposure to air. Do not soak them too long, however, as vitamins will be lost in the process.

Maincrop potatoes are prone to blackening after cooking. Prevent this by adding a squeeze of lemon juice or a teaspoon of vinegar to the cooking water.

In terms of retaining nutrients and flavour, steaming is a better method for cooking potatoes than boiling, although it does take a little longer. To peel hot potatoes after boiling or steaming, hold

Cooking Methods

them in a tea towel and remove the skins with a potato peeler. However, this can be a painful and tedious process and is not recommended if you are preparing potatoes for more than two or three people.

Serve boiled or steamed potatoes, with or without their skins, plain or jazzed up with a pat of savoury butter or a tasty pesto.

Mashing

There are various different ways of making mash but the basic principles are the same. Cut the potatoes into similarly sized pieces so that they cook evenly, then boil or steam them as above. Drain thoroughly. Peel the potatoes if they were cooked in their skins, then mash until smooth. If the basic potato mash is too watery, dry it off in the pan before proceeding. Add butter and warm, not cold, milk and beat until fluffy. Season to taste and serve.

The character of mash depends on the texture of the potatoes used – whether they are floury or waxy. Any variety of potato can be used. Floury varieties produce a fluffier mash, while waxy potatoes produce a denser, richer version, inclined to go a little gluey.

Mash can be stiff or soft; it can be made using a potato masher or roughly with a fork, or whipped until light with a hand whisk. Whizzing it in a blender or food processor will produce a purée – runnier than mash, and smooth like a thick cream sauce. Mash or purée can also be made by passing cooked potatoes through a food mill or potato ricer. While traditional mash made with butter and milk is smooth, light and fluffy, modern mash may be made with olive oil.

Serve mash just as it is or pile it into a shallow heatproof dish, fork up the top and brown under a grill. Mash reheats well but does not freeze. Leftover mash can be used as the basis for other recipes, for example in potato pastry, fish cakes or bread making.

Baking

Baked, or jacket, potatoes are a big favourite. Baking retains the goodness and flavour of potatoes since these are not lost in boiling water. Although any variety can be baked, the best potatoes for baking are floury varieties. The potato becomes fluffy inside as its starch expands under the intense heat.

Scrub potatoes for baking then pat dry. Carefully cut away any damaged parts and prick the skins with a fork or sharp knife. This allows steam to escape during cooking and prevents the potatoes from exploding or bursting apart. To produce very crisp skins, brush the potatoes with oil and sprinkle with salt. If you prefer a soft skin, wrap each potato in a square of foil.

Place the potatoes directly on an oven shelf and bake at 200°C (400°F), Gas Mark 6, for about 1–1½ hours, depending on their size, until tender right through. To check if the potatoes are cooked, squeeze gently – they should feel soft to the touch – or pierce with a skewer or sharp knife.

If you are short of time for cooking the potatoes, cut them in half lengthways and brush the cut surface with olive oil. This will reduce the cooking time by up to half. Using a potato baker, which has metal prongs to spear through the potatoes and which help conduct the heat more quickly, will also reduce the cooking time. Simply pushing a metal skewer through each potato before baking has the same effect.

Potatoes can also be 'baked' using a microwave oven. Wash, dry and prick the potatoes as usual and wrap each one in absorbent kitchen paper. Cook on 'high' for 5–6 minutes for one potato, 10–12 minutes for two or 18–20 minutes for four. Microwaving produces a cooked potato with a soft skin, which is quite different from a conventionally baked potato, but tastes good and is great when time is a consideration.

Cooking Methods

Serve baked potatoes straight from the oven, split open and smothered with butter, or scoop out the flesh, mix it with other ingredients such as tapenade or a soft creamy cheese and pile it back into the skins.

To bake new potatoes, cut them in half and place on a large piece of buttered foil. Sprinkle with salt and pepper, seal the foil and place on a baking sheet. Cook in a preheated oven, 180°C (350°F), Gas Mark 4, for about 1 hour.

Roasting

A perfect roast potato should never be greasy. It should be dry and crisp on the outside and soft and fluffy inside. The desired crunchy and uneven, rather than smooth, surface of roast potatoes is achieved by parboiling the potatoes first then roughing up their exteriors with a fork. Roast potatoes should not sit around after cooking, but are best eaten straight from the oven, before they lose their crunchiness.

Use either type of potato for roasting – a floury one produces a fluffy inside, a waxy potato gives a soft smooth inside. Parboil the potatoes for 5 minutes, then drain thoroughly. Return to the dry saucepan and shake them against the sides of the pan to roughen the exteriors or score them with a fork. Allow to cool. Heat a little oil in a shallow ovenproof dish or roasting tin, then add the parboiled roughened potatoes and turn them in the sizzling oil to coat them well. Roast at 190°C (375°F), Gas Mark 5 for 45–60 minutes, basting the potatoes regularly and turning them once or twice.

The traditional way to roast potatoes is around the meat joint but roasting them in a separate shallow dish avoids juices from the joint making the potatoes soggy. Add herbs such as rosemary and/or garlic to add flavour to the roasting potatoes, if liked. Another option is to roast them in oil for 30 minutes as above, then pour off any visible fat from the dish and continue cooking them by dry-roasting for another 15 minutes or so, until cooked through and golden brown and crunchy on the outside. Serve immediately, sprinkled with salt.

Deep-frying

To make chips, peel potatoes and cut them into thick slices, then into sticks. Leave the chipped potatoes in a large bowl of cold water for about 30 minutes to remove excess starch, otherwise they will stick together when they are fried. Drain them and pat them dry well, using a tea towel or kitchen paper. It is very important to dry the potatoes thoroughly before frying them, or the hot fat will foam up over the wet potatoes and could easily bubble over.

Using a deep-fat fryer, heat the oil to 190°C (375°F), or until a chip dropped in rises to the surface immediately, surrounded by bubbles. Quarter-fill the frying basket with chips, lower it into the oil and cook for 6–7 minutes, until the chips are soft but not browned. Raise the basket to drain the chips; repeat with the rest of the potatoes. Fry all the chips for a second time, for 3 minutes, until golden and crisp. Drain and serve.

Game chips are peeled potatoes cut into wafer-thin slices, then deep-fried until golden and drained on kitchen paper.

Sautéing

Use a firm-fleshed, waxy variety of potato for sautéing. Parboil the potatoes for 10 minutes, until barely tender. Drain, peel and cut into slices or large chunks. Heat unsalted or clarified butter and oil together in a wide shallow heavy-bottomed frying pan until hot and foaming. Add the potatoes and sauté gently until golden and crisp all over. Drain on kitchen paper, sprinkle with salt and serve.

Gratins

Served in the dish in which it is cooked, a good gratin is made by layering waxy potatoes with cream in a shallow ovenproof dish and cooking them slowly in the oven. The potato slices on top become crisp and golden, hiding a rich

creamy centre beneath. The use of a
shallow dish ensures that every serving
receives some of the crusty top, which
may be enhanced by a sprinkling of
breadcrumbs or grated cheese, such as
Gruyère or Parmesan.

Griddling

Both new and sweet potatoes can be
griddled, and its characteristic scorch
marks and smoky flavour gives them the
look and taste of food cooked over an
outdoor barbecue. Slices of peeled
sweet potatoes will take about 8–10
minutes each side to griddle. Griddle
small new potatoes, halved lengthways,
for 10 minutes on each side.

Barbecueing

A barbecue can be unreliable for baking
potatoes in their skins, so it is best to
bake them conventionally first for about
30 minutes (see above), then wrap them
in foil and place in the hot ashes around
the edges of the barbecue or bonfire to
finish cooking.

To barbecue new potatoes, first boil
them in their skins until they are just
cooked. Thread them on to skewers
(presoaked if wooden, to prevent them
from burning), brush them with oil and
season with salt and pepper. Barbecue
the skewered potatoes about for 5–10
minutes, until the skins are crisp, turning
them frequently.

Basic Techniques and Recipes

Spatchcocking a Poussin

A spatchcocked poussin looks impressive and cooks quickly, making it great for barbecues. Although spatchcocked poussin has become a regular item on supermarket shelves, there is no reason why this relatively simple job cannot be done at home. As well as the usual sharp knife, you will need one pair of long skewers per bird. If using wooden skewers, soak them in water for 30 minutes before use to prevent them burning during cooking.

1. Put the poussin, breast-side down, on a chopping board, Cut along each side of the backbone (poultry shears are ideal for this) and discard it.
2. Open out the bird and cut the wishbone in half. Turn the bird over so that it is breast-side up on the board and push down on it hard with the heel of your hand to break the breastbone and flatten it.
3. Trim off the ends of the wings. Cut a slit in the skin between the breastbone and each leg and tuck the ends of the legs into the slit.
4. To keep the bird flat as it cooks, thread the wooden skewers across the bird through both wings and legs. Wipe the bird with kitchen paper.

Makes approx. 100 ml (3½ fl oz) / Preparation time: 3 minutes

Harissa

Harissa is a fiery red, spicy hot chilli paste, made from red peppers, chillies, garlic and spices and used in North African cooking.

2 red peppers, roasted and skinned
25 g (1 oz) fresh red chillies, chopped, seeds retained
1–2 garlic cloves, crushed
½ teaspoon coriander seeds, toasted
2 teaspoons caraway seeds
olive oil
salt

1. Put the red peppers, the chillies and their seeds, garlic, coriander and caraway seeds and a pinch of salt in a blender or food processor and mix together, adding enough oil to make a thick paste.
2. Pack the harissa into a small, clean, dry jar and pour a layer of oil over the top. Cover with a tight-fitting lid and keep in the refrigerator.

Makes approx. 275 ml (9 fl oz) / Preparation time: 10 minutes

Aïoli

2 egg yolks
2–8 garlic cloves, crushed
½ teaspoon sea salt
1 tablespoon white wine vinegar
300 ml (½ pint) olive oil
pepper

1. Combine all the ingredients except the oil in a blender or food processor, season with pepper and process briefly until pale and creamy.
2. With the motor running, gradually pour in the oil through the funnel until the mixture is thick, glossy and pale. You may need to add a little boiling water to the mixture if it becomes too thick.
3. Transfer the mixture to a bowl and taste and adjust the seasoning, if necessary. Cover with cling film and refrigerate until required. The aïoli will keep for up to 3 days.

Soups

Potato Soup with Parsley

1.5 litres (2½ pints) beef stock

4 potatoes, peeled and coarsely grated

1 egg yolk

1 hard-boiled egg yolk, mashed

50 ml (2 fl oz) single cream

50 g (2 oz) Parmesan cheese, freshly grated

1 tablespoon finely chopped parsley

salt and pepper

croûtons, to serve (see below)

1. Place the beef stock in a large saucepan and bring to the boil. Sprinkle the grated potatoes with salt and pepper then drop them into the boiling stock. Cook for about 15 minutes, stirring occasionally.
2. Place the egg yolk in a soup tureen, beat well then add the mashed hard-boiled egg yolk. Blend the single cream, Parmesan and finely chopped parsley into the egg mixture and whisk them together.
3. Carefully pour about 250 ml (8 fl oz) of the stock into the egg mixture. Reheat the remaining stock and potatoes and gradually add them to the soup tureen. Sprinkle with croûtons and serve warm.

TIP · To make croûtons, remove the crusts from 3 slices of bread. Using 4½ teaspoons of lemon juice, brush both sides of the bread slices with lemon juice. Toast the bread until pale brown on both sides. Cut into cubes or strips and serve.

Chilled Potato Chowder

5 potatoes, peeled and diced

3 onions, sliced

475 g (15 oz) can cream of mushroom soup

25 g (1 oz) butter or margarine

900 ml (1½ pints) milk

1 teaspoon prepared English mustard

salt and pepper

To garnish:

2 tablespoons cottage cheese

a few snipped chives

paprika

1. Place the potatoes and onions in a large saucepan. Add just enough water to cover and cook the vegetables until tender. Drain the vegetables, then rub them through a coarse sieve into a clean saucepan.

2. Add the mushroom soup, butter or margarine, milk and mustard, with salt and pepper to taste. Stir well. Heat gently until the soup begins to simmer. Pour the soup into a bowl and leave to cool.

3. Cover the bowl closely and place the chowder in the refrigerator for at least 3 hours.

4. Serve the soup in chilled bowls, garnishing each serving with a little cottage cheese, a few snipped chives and a light dusting of paprika.

Serves 4–6 / Preparation time: 15 minutes / Cooking time: about 30 minutes

Curried Apple and Potato Soup

50 g (2 oz) butter or margarine

1 small onion, chopped

2 dessert apples, peeled, cored and sliced

1 tablespoon medium hot curry powder

600 ml (1 pint) vegetable stock

300 g (10 oz) potatoes, peeled and sliced

300 ml (½ pint) hot milk

salt

To garnish:

15 g (½ oz) butter

2–3 apple quarters, thinly sliced

cayenne pepper

1. Melt the butter or margarine in a saucepan and cook the chopped onion, stirring frequently, for 4–5 minutes, or until softened. Add the apples and curry powder and cook for a further 2 minutes, stirring.
2. Pour in the vegetable stock, then add the potatoes. Bring the mixture to the boil, lower the heat and simmer for 15–18 minutes, or until the apples and potatoes are very soft.
3. Using a blender or food processor, purée the mixture, in batches, until very smooth, then transfer to a clean saucepan. Reheat the purée and stir in the hot milk. Taste and adjust the seasoning if necessary.
4. While the soup is reheating, melt the butter for the garnish in a small frying pan, add the sliced apple to the pan and sauté until crisp.
5. Serve the soup in warmed bowls, garnishing each serving with the sautéed apple and a light sprinkling of cayenne pepper.

Serves 6–8 / Preparation time: 20 minutes / Cooking time: about 30 minutes

Gruyère Soup with Bacon and Potatoes

2 tablespoons olive oil

3 rashers of rindless smoked bacon, chopped

2 onions, finely chopped

600 ml (1 pint) chicken stock

900 ml (1½ pints) water

625 g (1¼ lb) potatoes, peeled and cut into
   1 cm (½ inch) cubes

4 tablespoons plain flour

50 g (2 oz) Gruyère cheese, grated

1 tablespoon medium dry sherry

1 teaspoon Worcestershire sauce

3 tablespoons finely chopped parsley

pepper

1. Heat the oil in a saucepan and cook the bacon and onions over a moderate heat until the onion is pale golden. Add the chicken stock, 600 ml (1 pint) of the water and the potatoes. Bring the mixture to the boil, then lower the heat, cover the pan and simmer for 15 minutes, or until the potatoes are tender.
2. In a small bowl whisk the flour with the remaining 300 ml (½ pint) water, then stir it into the soup. Cook, covered, for 5 minutes, stirring frequently.
3. In a blender or food processor, blend the grated Gruyère with 300 ml (½ pint) of the soup. Stir this purée back into the rest of the soup, then add the sherry and Worcestershire sauce with pepper, to taste. Simmer for 3–5 minutes.
4. Serve immediately or cool, cover and place in the refrigerator for up to 3 days. Heat thoroughly before serving, stirring in the parsley at the last moment.

Prawn Vichyssoise

This sophisticated iced soup is made from some very humble ingredients – leeks and potatoes. It can be prepared 24 hours in advance and must be velvety smooth and well chilled.

1 kg (2 lb) leeks, trimmed and cleaned

50 g (2 oz) butter or margarine

1 onion, chopped

1 litre (1¾ pints) chicken or vegetable stock

pinch of ground nutmeg

750 g (1½ lb) floury potatoes, peeled and cubed

600 ml (1 pint) milk

300 ml (½ pint) single cream

175 g (6 oz) cooked peeled prawns

150 ml (¼ pint) double cream, chilled

salt and pepper

trimmed chives, to garnish

1. Slice off the green tops of the leeks and reserve for use in another recipe. Slice the white parts of the leeks thinly.

2. Melt the butter or margarine in a large saucepan. Add the leeks and onion and cook over a moderate heat for 5 minutes, stirring constantly. Do not allow the vegetables to change colour.

3. Add the stock, nutmeg and potatoes, with salt and pepper to taste. Bring the mixture to the boil, lower the heat and cook, partially covered, for 25 minutes. Pour in the milk and simmer for a further 5–8 minutes. Cool slightly.

4. Using a blender or food processor, purée the mixture, in batches, until smooth, then rub it through a sieve into a bowl. Add the single cream. Stir well and cover the bowl closely. Chill in the refrigerator for at least 3 hours. Just before serving, stir in the prawns, swirl in the double cream and add more salt and pepper if required.

5. Serve the soup in chilled bowls, garnishing each serving with a generous sprinkling of chives.

FOOD FACT Vichyssoise was originally a chilled potato and leek cream soup created in the early 20th century by a French chef, who came from near Vichy in France. The name vichyssoise is often now given to any cold vegetable soup based on potatoes.

Serves 8 / Preparation time: 20 minutes / Cooking time: 55 minutes

Potato and Bacon Soup

1. Cut the rinds off the bacon and set them aside. Roughly chop the bacon rashers.
2. Heat the oil in a large saucepan and cook the bacon rinds over a medium heat until crisp, then remove them with a slotted spoon and discard.
3. Add the chopped bacon, onion and garlic to the fat in the pan and cook over a medium heat, stirring frequently, for 8–10 minutes, or until the onion is light brown and the bacon fairly crisp.
4. Add the stock, water, potatoes, leeks, marjoram, nutmeg and Worcestershire sauce to the pan, with pepper to taste. Bring the mixture to the boil, lower the heat, cover and simmer for 25 minutes, stirring occasionally.
5. Put 600 ml (1 pint) of the soup mixture in a blender or food processor and process for about 2 seconds, until roughly blended. Alternatively, mash with a potato masher.
6. Return the mixture to the saucepan, stir well and cook the soup for 10 minutes over a low heat. Add salt to taste. Just before serving stir in the parsley, if using. Serve in warmed soup bowls.

175 g (6 oz) smoked bacon rashers with rinds

1 tablespoon olive oil

1 onion, finely chopped

2 garlic cloves, finely chopped

600 ml (1 pint) chicken stock

1.2 litres (2 pints) water

750 g (1½ lb) potatoes, peeled and diced

3 leeks, trimmed, cleaned and sliced

1 teaspoon chopped marjoram

½ teaspoon ground nutmeg

1 teaspoon Worcestershire sauce

3–4 tablespoons finely chopped flat leaf parsley (optional)

salt and pepper

Serves 4 / Preparation time: 20 minutes, plus preparing the lobsters / Cooking time: 1 hour

Lobster and Corn Chowder

2 cooked lobsters, 750 g (1½ lb) each

25 g (1 oz) butter

1 onion, finely chopped

1 carrot, finely chopped

1 celery stick, finely chopped

1 sprig of thyme

1 sprig of parsley

2 bay leaves

1 litre (1¾ pints) water

Chowder:

200 g (7 oz) can sweetcorn kernels, drained

25 g (1 oz) butter

1 small onion, chopped

1 small garlic clove, crushed

50 g (2 oz) pancetta, cut into small strips

300 ml (½ pint) milk

300 ml (½ pint) single cream

1 kg (2 lb) potatoes, peeled and cut into
 1.5 cm (¾ inch) cubes

cayenne pepper

4 tomatoes, skinned, deseeded and chopped

salt and pepper

1. Cut the lobsters in half lengthways, remove and discard the greyish-green tomalley (the liver), the gills and the intestinal vein running along the back. Smash the claws and remove the meat. Cut up the remaining meat. Place the shells in a plastic bag and smash into small pieces with a rolling pin.

2. Place the butter in a large saucepan and melt over a low heat. Add the onion, carrot and celery and cook for 8–10 minutes, until soft.

3. Add the fresh herbs, water and pieces of lobster shell. Bring to the boil, lower the heat and simmer for 30 minutes. Strain through a fine sieve.

4. To make the chowder, place two-thirds of the sweetcorn in a blender or food processor with the strained lobster broth and work until smooth. Melt the butter in a large flameproof casserole, add the onion and garlic and cook gently for 5 minutes.

5. Add the pancetta and cook until golden. Add the puréed sweetcorn mixture, the milk, cream, potatoes and remaining sweetcorn. Bring to the boil, lower the heat and simmer for 10–15 minutes, until the potatoes are tender.

6. Season with salt, pepper and cayenne. Stir in the chopped tomatoes and lobster meat. Heat through and serve.

FOOD FACT Fresh lobsters are available all year but are at their best and most plentiful in summer. They are generally available cooked and ready to eat. However, lobster flesh toughens easily so unless it has been cooked very carefully, it may be a rubbery disappointment. Of a lobster's total weight, about one-quarter is edible meat.

Serves 6–8 / Preparation time: 20 minutes / Cooking time: 1 hour

Sweet Potato Soup

25 g (1 oz) butter or margarine

1 onion, chopped

2 carrots, sliced

2 celery sticks, sliced

1 bay leaf

750 g (1½ lb) sweet potatoes, peeled and sliced

250 g (8 oz) potatoes, peeled and sliced

1.2 litres (2 pints) chicken stock

150 ml (¼ pint) water

125 ml (4 fl oz) dry white wine

¼ teaspoon grated nutmeg

¼ teaspoon white pepper

4–6 rashers of rindless smoked bacon

salt

chopped parsley, to garnish

1. Heat the butter or margarine in a frying pan and cook the onion, carrots, celery and bay leaf over a low heat for 5–8 minutes, stirring often.
2. Transfer the mixture to a saucepan. Add the sweet potatoes, potatoes, stock, water and white wine. Bring the mixture to the boil, then lower the heat and simmer, uncovered, for about 35–40 minutes, or until the vegetables are very tender. Remove the bay leaf.
3. Heat the bacon in a frying pan over a gentle heat until the fat runs, then raise the heat and fry over a moderate heat until very crisp. Using tongs, transfer the bacon on to kitchen paper to drain.
4. In a blender or food processor, blend the mixture, in batches, until smooth, transferring each successive batch to a clean saucepan. Add the nutmeg, white pepper and salt to taste. Place the pan over a moderate heat, and stir until the soup is hot.
5. Serve the soup in warmed bowls. Cut each bacon rasher into 2–3 pieces and divide among the bowls to garnish.

Serves 4–6 / Preparation time: 15 minutes / Cooking time: 40 minutes

Leek and Potato Soup

25 g (1 oz) butter

2 large leeks, trimmed, cleaned and finely sliced

250 g (8 oz) potatoes, peeled and roughly diced

1 onion, roughly chopped

750 ml (1¼ pints) chicken stock or water

300 ml (½ pint) milk

salt and pepper

1 tablespoon snipped chives, to garnish

1. Melt the butter in a large saucepan, add the leeks, potatoes and onion. Stir well to coat with the butter. Cover tightly with a piece of greaseproof paper and cook over a very gentle heat for about 15 minutes, until the vegetables have softened, stirring frequently, to prevent them from browning.

2. Add the chicken stock or water and milk and season with salt and pepper. Bring to the boil, lower the heat and simmer gently for about 20 minutes until the vegetables are tender.

3. Using a blender or food processor, purée the mixture in batches until smooth, and transfer to a clean saucepan.

4. Adjust the seasoning if necessary and heat until very hot, then pour the soup into individual warmed bowls. Garnish with chives and serve.

Serves 4–6 / Preparation time: 20 minutes / Cooking time: 50–55 minutes

Red Pepper and Potato Soup

3 tablespoons olive oil

1 garlic clove, chopped

1 onion, chopped

2 red peppers, cored, deseeded and chopped

1.2 litres (2 pints) vegetable stock

½ teaspoon finely chopped fresh rosemary
   or ¼ teaspoon dried rosemary

¼ teaspoon sugar

2 tablespoons tomato purée

250 g (8 oz) potatoes, peeled and chopped

salt and pepper

1. Heat the olive oil in a large saucepan. Add the garlic, onion and red peppers and fry for 5 minutes, stirring frequently.

2. Add the vegetable stock, rosemary, sugar and tomato purée. Stir well, then add the potatoes. Bring the mixture to the boil, lower the heat and simmer, partially covered, for 40–45 minutes, or until the vegetables are very soft.

3. Using a blender or food processor, purée the mixture, in batches, until very smooth then transfer to a clean saucepan. Season with salt and pepper. Reheat gently and serve in warmed soup bowls.

Serves 6 / Preparation time: 15 minutes / Cooking time: 40 minutes

Caldo Verde

2 tablespoons olive oil

1 large onion, chopped

2 garlic cloves, chopped

500 g (1 lb) potatoes, peeled and cut into
   2.5 cm (1 inch) cubes

1.2 litres (2 pints) water or vegetable stock

250 g (8 oz) spring greens, finely shredded

2 tablespoons chopped parsley

salt and pepper

croûtons, to serve (see page 24)

1. Heat the olive oil in a large frying pan and fry the onion for 5 minutes, until softened but not brown. Add the garlic and potatoes and cook for a few minutes, stirring occasionally.
2. Add the water or stock, season with salt and pepper, to taste, and cook for 15 minutes, until the potatoes are tender.
3. Mash the potatoes roughly in their liquid, then add the spring greens and boil, uncovered, for 10 minutes.
4. Add the parsley and simmer for 2–3 minutes, until heated through. Serve the soup with croûtons.

FOOD FACT Like many green vegetables, spring greens contain folic acid, or folate. Folate is necessary for normal cell growth and for the prevention of a particular form of anaemia. The folate content of foods diminishes with storage, so choose leafy vegetables that are as fresh as possible.

2) Salads

Potato Salad with Dill Pickle and Anchovy

750 g (1½ lb) waxy salad potatoes, scrubbed
4 spring onions, finely chopped
1 dill pickle, finely sliced
salt and pepper

Dressing:
6 tablespoons mayonnaise
3 tablespoons single cream
1 teaspoon Dijon mustard

To garnish:
anchovy fillets or strips of canned or
    bottled pimiento
2 tablespoons snipped chives

1. Cook the potatoes, whole and in their skins, in a large saucepan of boiling water for 10–15 minutes, or until tender. Drain and refresh under cold running water, then drain thoroughly and leave to cool.
2. Thickly slice the potatoes and place in a serving bowl with the chopped spring onions and dill pickle. Add salt and pepper to taste.
3. To make the dressing, mix the mayonnaise, single cream and mustard together in a small bowl. Spoon the dressing over the potatoes and toss lightly to mix.
4. Serve the salad garnished with anchovy fillets or strips of pimiento and sprinkled with the snipped chives.

Hot Potato Salad with Feta and Caper Vinaigrette

750 g (1½ lb) small red-skinned
  potatoes, scrubbed
125 g (4 oz) feta cheese, crumbled

Caper vinaigrette:
1 tablespoon sherry vinegar
1½ teaspoons Dijon mustard
2 tablespoons capers, drained and
  roughly chopped
1 tablespoon chopped tarragon
6 tablespoons extra virgin olive oil
salt and pepper

1. Cook the potatoes in a large saucepan of lightly salted boiling water for 10–15 minutes, or until just tender. Drain well. Cut the potatoes in half, if large.

2. To make the caper vinaigrette, mix together the vinegar, mustard, capers and tarragon in a small bowl. Using a balloon whisk, gradually whisk in the olive oil in a steady stream until amalgamated and season with salt and pepper.

3. Toss the warm potatoes with the vinaigrette and sprinkle with the crumbled feta.

FOOD FACT · Capers are the small, green, unopened flower buds of a Mediterranean shrub. They are used, pickled, as a flavouring and as a garnish and are an essential ingredient in both Italian and Provençal cooking. They have a characteristic and slightly bitter flavour, which is developed by pickling.

Serves 2 as a main course / Preparation time: 15 minutes / Cooking time: 30 minutes

Warm Salade Niçoise

It is impossible to give a definitive recipe for Salade Niçoise as there is much controversy as to what can and cannot be included in an authentic one. This one will be greeted with horror by any traditionalists, but it does make a very good dish.

about 250 g (8 oz) small new potatoes,
    scrubbed, or medium potatoes, scrubbed
    and quartered

5 tablespoons virgin olive oil

2 tablespoons red wine vinegar

250 g (8 oz) French beans

250 g (8 oz) fresh tuna steak, cut into
    finger strips

2 garlic cloves, finely chopped

2 anchovy fillets, chopped

about 1½ teaspoons Dijon mustard

1 red pepper, charred, skinned, cored, deseeded
    and thinly sliced

2 tablespoons capers

salt and pepper

lemon wedges, to garnish (optional)

1. Steam the potatoes in a colander set over a saucepan of boiling water for about 15–20 minutes, or until just tender. Transfer to a serving bowl and toss gently with 1 tablespoon each of the olive oil and red wine vinegar, and salt and pepper.
2. Steam the French beans in the same way for 5–6 minutes, until just tender. Set aside.
3. Heat another 1 tablespoon of the oil in a nonstick frying pan, add the strips of tuna and sear evenly over a high heat. Add to the potato mixture.
4. Add the remaining olive oil to the frying pan, then stir in the garlic and anchovies for 30 seconds. Stir in the remaining vinegar and boil for about 1 minute. Stir in the mustard, then pour over the potato mixture.
5. Add the pepper strips, steamed beans, capers and more black pepper to the salad. Toss gently, taste and adjust the seasoning, if necessary. Serve immediately, garnished with lemon wedges, if liked.

New Potato and Celery Salad

500 g (1 lb) small Jersey Royal potatoes,
   scrubbed
6 celery sticks, with leaves if possible
75 g (3 oz) black olives
3 tablespoons capers, rinsed and drained
few sprigs of parsley, roughly chopped
salt and pepper

Tarragon and lemon dressing:
2 tablespoons tarragon vinegar
1 teaspoon finely grated lemon rind
¼ teaspoon Dijon mustard
1 tablespoon chopped tarragon
5 tablespoons olive oil or grapeseed oil

1. Cook the potatoes in a large saucepan of lightly salted boiling water for 10–15 minutes, until just tender. Drain and refresh under cold running water, then drain thoroughly and leave to cool.
2. Slice the celery sticks diagonally and roughly chop any leaves. Place in a bowl with the olives, capers and parsley. Add the cooled potatoes and season with salt and pepper.
3. To make the dressing, combine the vinegar, lemon rind, mustard and tarragon in a small bowl. Add salt and pepper to taste. Stir to mix, then gradually whisk in the oil, using a balloon whisk. Alternatively, mix all the ingredients in a screw-top jar, close the lid tightly and shake well to combine.
4. Pour the dressing over the salad, toss well and serve.

Serves 4 / Preparation time: 15 minutes / Cooking time: about 1 hour / Oven temperature: 200°C (400°F), Gas Mark 6

Warm Potato and Pancetta Salad

This aromatic potato salad is delicious on its own, or as a side dish, or perhaps with one or two other root vegetable salads. When you cut the onions into wedges, leave the root ends intact so that the layers do not separate.

500 g (1 lb) small new potatoes, scrubbed

2 red onions, cut into wedges, roots left intact

4 sprigs of rosemary, plus extra to garnish

6 tablespoons extra virgin olive oil

75 g (3 oz) smoked pancetta, in thick slices, cut into strips

3 tablespoons red wine vinegar

coarse sea salt and pepper

1. Parboil the potatoes in a large saucepan of boiling water for 5 minutes. Drain thoroughly and transfer to a roasting tin.

2. Add the red onion wedges to the roasting tin with the sprigs of rosemary. Drizzle over 4 tablespoons of the olive oil.

3. Place the roasting tin in a preheated oven, 200°C (400°F), Gas Mark 6, and roast for 45 minutes–1 hour, until the potatoes are tender and lightly patched with brown.

4. When the potatoes are cooked, heat the remaining 2 tablespoons of olive oil in a frying pan. Add the pancetta and fry until crisp and lightly browned. Add the red wine vinegar and bring to the boil, stirring, to deglaze the pan. Pour over the potatoes and toss to coat. Season with coarse sea salt and pepper.

5. Serve warm or cold, discarding the cooked rosemary stalks just before serving, and adding a few fresh sprigs to garnish.

FOOD FACT Pancetta is cured belly of pork; it is evenly pink and white in colour and may be smoked or, more usually, air-dried and salt-cured. It must be cooked before eating. It is an important ingredient in Italian cuisine and there are many regional variations. Pancetta is widely used in pasta sauces, risottos and bean casseroles.

Sweet Potato and Grilled Chilli Salad

750 g (1½ lb) sweet potatoes, washed, peeled or
   unpeeled and sliced

3 large fresh red chillies

6 tablespoons groundnut oil, for frying

handful of coriander leaves, torn

coarse sea salt and pepper

50 g (2 oz) lamb's lettuce or rocket, to serve

Dressing:

1 teaspoon finely grated lime rind

2 tablespoons lime juice

4 tablespoons groundnut oil

2 tablespoons sesame oil

1. Parboil the sweet potato slices in a large saucepan of boiling water for 5 minutes. Drain the potatoes well, then refresh under cold running water. Spread out on kitchen paper to dry.
2. Meanwhile, cook the chillies under a preheated hot grill, turning them frequently, until the skins are blistered and blackened all over. Leave to cool slightly, then carefully remove and discard the skin and seeds. Cut the flesh into thin strips and set aside.
3. Heat 3 tablespoons of the groundnut oil in a large frying pan. Sauté the sweet potato slices in batches over a medium-high heat until crisp and lightly browned. Transfer to a large shallow serving bowl as they are done and add more oil to the pan as necessary.
4. To make the dressing, mix all the ingredients together in a small bowl until thoroughly blended or shake together in a screw-top jar.
5. Add the strips of chilli and the torn coriander leaves to the salad bowl. Season with coarse sea salt and pepper, to taste. Toss lightly to mix.
6. Just before serving, pour the dressing over the sweet potatoes and chilli and toss well. Serve with lamb's lettuce or rocket.

3) Mashed Potatoes

Serves 4 / Preparation time: 15 minutes / Cooking time: 20–25 minutes

Champ

Champ, also known as cally, poundies and pandy, is one of the most famous ways of serving Ireland's best loved vegetable – the potato. Traditionally, champ would have been served as a main meal, with a glass of milk or buttermilk. Nowadays, however, it is used to accompany meats such as boiled ham and grilled sausages. Parsley, young nettle tops, peas and broad beans can be substituted for the spring onions.

1 kg (2 lb) potatoes, left unpeeled
150 ml (¼ pint) milk
4–5 spring onions, finely chopped, plus extra,
 to garnish
50–125 g (2–4 oz) butter
salt and pepper

1. Cook the potatoes in a large saucepan of boiling water for about 20 minutes, or until tender.
2. Meanwhile, put the milk and chopped spring onions into a saucepan. Bring to the boil and simmer for a few minutes. Keep warm.
3. When the potatoes are cooked, drain them and return to the pan. Dry them over a low heat, covered with a piece of kitchen paper. Then, holding the warm potatoes in a tea towel, peel them carefully and mash well using a potato masher or fork.
4. Gradually beat the spring onion-flavoured milk into the mashed potatoes to form a soft but not sloppy mixture. Beat in half the butter and season with salt and pepper.
5. Divide the potatoes between 4 warmed plates or bowls and make a well in the centre of each serving. Cut the remaining butter into four and put a piece in each of the servings. Garnish with spring onions and serve immediately.

Serves 4 / Preparation time: 10 minutes / Cooking time: 20 minutes

Creamy mashed potatoes

Choose old, floury potatoes. When cooked sufficiently, the potatoes should break under the pressure of a fork but not be mushy. Overcooking or cutting potatoes into small pieces makes them water-soaked and they lose flavour. Add hot milk for fluffy potatoes as cold milk makes them sticky.

6 potatoes, peeled
50 g (2 oz) butter
125–250 ml (4–8 fl oz) hot milk
freshly grated nutmeg (optional)
salt and pepper

1. Cook the potatoes in a large saucepan of lightly salted boiling water until they are easily pierced with a skewer – about 20 minutes.
2. Drain, return to the saucepan and shake the pan over a low heat for a few minutes until the potatoes are thoroughly dry. Mash well with a potato masher or fork. Then, using a wooden spoon, beat until very smooth. Add the butter to the potatoes, then gradually beat in the hot milk until the potatoes are light and fluffy.
3. Season with salt and pepper, and a pinch of nutmeg, if liked.
4. To keep the potatoes hot after mashing, push them well down in the saucepan, packing the potato tightly. Level the top, add butter and spoon about 4 tablespoons hot milk over the top. Cover and leave in a warm place. Before serving beat well, adding more hot milk if necessary. The potatoes will keep like this for up to 20 minutes.

Serves 4 / Preparation time: 15 minutes / Cooking time: 20 minutes

Horseradish Mash

about 750 g (1½ lb) potatoes, peeled and cut
  into large chunks
50 g (2 oz) butter
150 ml (¼ pint) single cream
2–3 tablespoons freshly grated or prepared
  horseradish
salt and pepper

1. Cook the potatoes in a large saucepan
   of boiling water for about 20 minutes,
   or until tender.
2. Drain the potatoes well, then return to
   the pan. Add the butter, single cream
   and horseradish and mash well with a
   potato masher or fork. Season with salt
   and pepper to taste and serve.

Serves 4 / Preparation time: 20 minutes / Cooking time: 20–25 minutes

Mashed Potatoes with Garlic, Parsley and Olive Oil

Use firm, slightly waxy potatoes for this dish rather than the floury potato that is usually deemed essential for mashing. A firm, yellow potato such as Belle de Fontenay, is a good choice.

1 kg (2 lb) potatoes, left unpeeled
4 tablespoons extra virgin olive oil
4 tablespoons milk
3 large garlic cloves, crushed
4 tablespoons chopped flat leaf parsley
salt and pepper

1. Cook the potatoes in a large saucepan of boiling water for about 20 minutes, or until tender. Drain well. As soon as they are cool enough to handle, peel the potatoes, then allow them to dry out in a clean pan, stirring for a few moments, over a gentle heat.
2. Push the potatoes through a medium food mill back into the clean pan and stir over a very low heat to dry out further still.
3. Warm the olive oil and milk together in a small saucepan, then stir in the crushed garlic. Beat into the potato purée, adding plenty of salt and pepper. When the potato is smooth and well seasoned, stir in the chopped parsley and turn into a serving dish.

Serves 4 / Preparation time: 15 minutes / Cooking time: 40 minutes / Oven temperature: 160°C (325°F), Gas Mark 3

Roasted Garlic Mash

6 garlic cloves, left unpeeled

2 tablespoons olive oil

1 tablespoon finely chopped rosemary or thyme

3 baking potatoes, total weight about 750 g (1½ lb), unpeeled and cut into small chunks

50 g (2 oz) butter

125 ml (4 fl oz) milk

salt and pepper

1. Place the garlic cloves in a small ovenproof dish. Drizzle with the olive oil and sprinkle with the herbs. Cover with foil and bake in a preheated oven, 160°C (325°F), Gas Mark 3, for 35–40 minutes, until very soft.
2. Meanwhile, cook the potatoes in a large saucepan of boiling water for about 20 minutes, or until tender.
3. Remove the garlic from the oven and, when cooled, squeeze the cloves from their skins into a small bowl. Mash with a fork. Strain the oil from the dish through a sieve held over the garlic and mix well.
4. Combine the butter and milk in a small saucepan over a low heat and heat until the butter is melted. Drain the potatoes well when cooked, transfer to a warmed bowl and mash well with a potato masher or fork.
5. Add the butter mixture to the potatoes and stir until smooth. Stir in the mashed roasted garlic and season with salt and pepper, to taste.

Parmesan, Olive Oil and Pine Nut Mashed Potatoes

1.5 kg (3 lb) potatoes, such as Desirée, peeled
150 ml (¼ pint) olive oil, plus extra to serve
125 g (4 oz) freshly grated Parmesan cheese
50 g (2 oz) pine nuts, toasted, to serve

1. Boil the potatoes in salted water for 15–20 minutes, until very tender. Drain and leave to steam in the colander for 5 minutes.
2. Push the potatoes through a potato ricer or mash them by hand. With an electric whisk, beat in the olive oil, then the Parmesan. Continue beating for a few minutes over the heat so that the mash is nice and fluffy. Season well with salt and lots of pepper. Turn into a warmed serving dish, drizzle with more oil and scatter the pine nuts over the top.

Creamed Potatoes and Celeriac

1 kg (2 lb) potatoes, peeled and sliced

1 large celeriac, peeled and sliced

50 g (2 oz) butter, cut into small pieces

150 ml (¼ pint) soured cream or natural yogurt

salt and pepper

To garnish:

toasted flaked almonds

sprig of parsley

1. Cook the potatoes and the celeriac separately in large saucepans of lightly salted boiling water for about 20 minutes, or until tender. Drain well.

2. Purée the vegetables together using a blender or food processor or rub them through a sieve. Stir the pieces of butter into the hot vegetable purée. Blend in the soured cream or yogurt with plenty of freshly ground black pepper.

3. Put in a dish and serve garnished with toasted flaked almonds and a sprig of parsley. (This dish is ideal for making in advance and may be reheated just before serving in a bowl set over a saucepan of boiling water, or in a microwave oven.)

FOOD FACT Celeriac is the tuberous root of a plant belonging to the celery family. It has a milder sweeter taste than celery and is equally good cooked, or used raw in salads. It needs to be peeled but tends to discolour when cut – this can be prevented by adding a few drops of lemon juice to the cooking water, or to the salad if being used raw. When cooked, the texture of celeriac is similar to that of the potato, but with more bite to it.

Serves 4 / Preparation time: 15 minutes, plus infusing / Cooking time: 20 minutes

Saffron Mash

Many potato varieties are suitable for this side dish. Mashing baking potatoes yields fluffy results; for a smoother, creamier texture, use white or red new potatoes. The mash is shown here with a bowl of saffron water.

1 kg (2 lb) potatoes,
    peeled and cut into large chunks
100 ml (3½ fl oz) single cream
large pinch of saffron threads
2 tablespoons boiling water
5 tablespoons extra virgin olive oil
salt and pepper

1. Cook the potatoes in a large saucepan of boiling water for about 20 minutes, or until tender.
2. Meanwhile, heat the cream to simmering point in a small saucepan, then remove from the heat. Place the saffron in a small bowl with the boiling water and leave to infuse for 10 minutes.
3. When the potatoes are cooked, drain well, return to the pan and add the cream, saffron water and olive oil. Mash together well with a potato masher or fork, season with salt and pepper to taste and serve.

Serves 4–6 / Preparation time: 20 minutes / Cooking time: 20 minutes

Colcannon

Colcannon is similar to Champ (see page 54), but flavoured, coloured and textured by the addition of cooked and shredded kale, a member of the cabbage family.

500 g (1 lb) kale or green leaf cabbage, stalk
  removed, and finely shredded
500 g (1 lb) potatoes, unpeeled
6 spring onions or chives, finely chopped
150 ml (¼ pint) milk or single cream
125 g (4 oz) butter
salt and pepper

1. Place the kale or cabbage and the potatoes separately in large saucepans of lightly salted boiling water and cook until tender – about 10–20 minutes for the kale or cabbage, longer for the potatoes.
2. Meanwhile, place the spring onions or chives and the milk or cream in a small saucepan and simmer over a low heat for about 5 minutes.
3. Drain the kale or cabbage and mash with a fork.
4. Drain the potatoes. Holding them in a tea towel, peel them carefully while warm and mash well with a potato masher or fork. Add the hot milk and spring onions, beating well to give a soft fluffy texture. Beat in the mashed kale or cabbage, season with salt and pepper, to taste, and add half the butter. The colcannon should be a speckled, green colour.
5. Heat through thoroughly then serve in warmed individual dishes or bowls. Make a well in the centre of each serving and put a knob of the remaining butter in each one. Serve immediately.

VARIATION An alternative method is to purée the cooked kale in a blender or food processor along with the hot milk and spring onions before adding to the potatoes. This produces an even texture and overall green colour and makes an interesting variation.

4) Side Dishes

Serves 4 / Preparation time: 10 minutes / Cooking time: 25–30 minutes / Oven temperature: 230°C (450°F), Gas Mark 8

Roast Potatoes with Rosemary and Garlic

750 g (1½ lb) potatoes, unpeeled
4 tablespoons olive oil
2 tablespoons chopped rosemary
4 garlic cloves, sliced
salt and pepper
sprig of rosemary, to garnish

1. Cut the potatoes lengthways into quarters and pat dry with kitchen paper.
2. Put 2 tablespoons of the olive oil in a large roasting tin and place in a preheated oven, 230°C (450°F), Gas Mark 8, to warm through.
3. Mix together the remaining oil and the rosemary in a large bowl and toss the potatoes in the oil to coat them completely.
4. Add the potatoes to the roasting tin in the oven, shake carefully to ensure an even layer of potatoes, then place the tin at the top of the oven and roast for 20 minutes.
5. Remove the tin from the oven and move the potatoes around so that they cook evenly. Scatter the garlic among the potatoes, return the tin to the oven and cook for a further 5 minutes. Remove the potatoes from the oven, season with salt and pepper, garnish with a sprig of rosemary and serve immediately.

Serves 4 / Preparation time: 15 minutes / Cooking time: about 20 minutes

Almond Potatoes

375 g (12 oz) potatoes, cooked and mashed
   with milk and butter
seasoned flour, for coating
1 egg, beaten
125 g (4 oz) almonds, finely chopped
25 g (1 oz) butter
1 tablespoon sunflower oil

1. Divide the mashed potato into 12 pieces. Place the seasoned flour on a plate, the egg on
   another and the almonds on a third. Shape each portion of potato into a round cake,
   coating it with flour as you do so. Dip each potato cake in the beaten egg and then
   the almonds.
2. Heat the butter and oil together in a large frying pan and cook the potato cakes, a few at a
   time, for about 6 minutes, turning once, until golden. Drain on kitchen paper. Serve hot.

FOOD FACT Almonds are the seeds of a Mediterranean tree of the peach family, and one of the
most popular nuts worldwide. They have been cultivated since prehistoric times and
are the most important nut in commerce, with the USA being the main producer,
followed by Spain and Italy.

Serves 4–6 / Preparation time: 5 minutes / Cooking time: 55–60 minutes / Oven temperature: 220°C (425°F), Gas Mark 7

Chilli Chips

Use as little or as much chilli powder as you like,
to coat these oven-roasted potato chips.

4 large, even-sized potatoes
4–6 tablespoons olive oil
½ teaspoon salt
1–2 teaspoons chilli powder, or to taste
soured cream, mayonnaise or Aïoli
   (see page 21), to serve

1. Cut each potato into 8 wedges and
   place in a large bowl. Add the olive oil,
   salt and chilli powder and toss until
   evenly coated.
2. Transfer to a baking sheet and cook
   in a preheated oven, 220°C (425°F),
   Gas Mark 7, for 15 minutes. Turn over
   and cook for a further 15 minutes, then
   turn once more and cook for a final
   25–30 minutes, until crisp and golden.
3. Cool slightly and serve with either
   soured cream, mayonnaise or aïoli.

**Serves 2–4 / Preparation time: 15 minutes / Cooking time: 1–1¼ hours /
Oven temperature: 180°C (350°F), Gas Mark 4, then 200°C (400°F), Gas Mark 6**

Potatoes Dauphinoise

500 g (1 lb) potatoes, peeled and thinly sliced
40 g (1½ oz) butter
1 large garlic clove, crushed
300 ml (½ pint) double cream
salt and pepper
fresh red and green chillies, deseeded and
 finely sliced, to garnish (optional)
cooked French beans, to serve

1. Wash the sliced potatoes and pat dry
   with kitchen paper. Use the butter to
   grease an ovenproof dish. Scatter
   crushed garlic over the dish and fill with
   layers of potato slices.
2. Pour the cream over the potatoes and
   sprinkle with salt and pepper. Place the
   dish in a preheated oven, 180°C
   (350°F), Gas Mark 4, and bake for
   1–1¼ hours, or until the potatoes are
   tender when pierced with a skewer.
3. Increase the heat to 200°C (400°F),
   Gas Mark 6, for the last 10 minutes to
   brown the top.
4. Garnish with the chillies, if using, and
   serve hot with French beans.

Serves 4 / Preparation time: 20 minutes, plus soaking / Cooking time: 45 minutes / Oven temperature: 180°C (350°F), Gas Mark 4

Genoese Mushrooms and Potatoes

In this Ligurian recipe the potatoes absorb the flavour of the mushrooms, making it seem as if there are more mushrooms than there actually are.

20 g (¾ oz) dried ceps

300 ml (½ pint) hot water

375 g (12 oz) mushrooms, preferably chestnut, thinly sliced

500 g (1 lb) potatoes, peeled and thinly sliced

4 garlic cloves, crushed

leaves from a bunch of basil

olive oil, for brushing

salt and pepper

1. Soak the dried mushrooms in a bowl containing the hot water for 30 minutes. Drain off and strain the liquid through muslin or a filter paper. Simmer the rehydrated mushrooms in the strained soaking liquid until the liquid has evaporated. Toss with the fresh mushrooms, potatoes, garlic, basil and salt and pepper.

2. Oil an ovenproof dish that will hold the potatoes and mushrooms in a layer no more than about 3.5 cm (1½ inches) deep. Spread the vegetable mixture evenly in the dish.

3. Bake in a preheated oven, 180°C (350°F), Gas Mark 4, for about 45 minutes, until the potatoes are tender; turn the ingredients over about halfway through cooking. Leave to stand for a couple of minutes before serving.

Serves 4 / Preparation time: 15 minutes / Cooking time: 16–20 minutes

Potato Cakes

500 g (1 lb) potatoes, peeled
   and coarsely grated
1 onion, chopped
2 tablespoons chopped parsley
2 eggs, beaten
2 tablespoons olive oil
salt and pepper

1. Place the grated potatoes in a sieve and rinse well under cold running water to remove excess starch. Drain.
2. Place the potatoes in a bowl with the onion, parsley, eggs and salt and pepper to taste. Mix thoroughly and divide the mixture into equal rounds.
3. Heat the oil in a 20–23 cm (8–9 inch) heavy-based frying pan. Add the potato rounds, in batches, and pat lightly to shape into cakes. Fry the cakes gently for about 8–10 minutes, until the undersides are crisp and brown.
4. Carefully turn the cakes over and fry the other sides for 8–10 minutes, until crisp and brown.
5. Season with salt and pepper and serve immediately.

Serves 4 / Preparation time: 10 minutes, plus cooling / Cooking time: 40–45 minutes / Oven temperature: 200°C (400°F), Gas Mark 6

Roasted New Potatoes with Smoked Salmon and Caviar

This is a delicious combination, well worth the time spent assembling.

16 small new potatoes, about 40 g (1½ oz) each, scrubbed but unpeeled

2 tablespoons olive oil

1 tablespoon chopped rosemary

1 tablespoon chopped sage

125 g (4 oz) créme fraîche

125 g (4 oz) smoked salmon, cut into strips

25 g (1 oz) lumpfish caviar

1 tablespoon snipped chives

sea salt and pepper

lemon wedges, to serve (optional)

1. Place the potatoes in a roasting tin, add the olive oil, herbs and some sea salt and toss well. Put the roasting tin on the top shelf of a preheated oven, 200°C (400°F), Gas Mark 6, and roast for 40–45 minutes, stirring occasionally, until the potatoes are crisp on the outside and very soft in the centre.

2. Remove the potatoes from the oven and leave to cool for 5 minutes.

3. Cut a cross in the top of each potato and press open slightly. Transfer to a serving plate and top each with a spoonful of crème fraîche, a piece of smoked salmon, a little caviar and snipped chives.

4. Serve immediately with plenty of freshly ground black pepper and lemon wedges, if liked.

Emmental Potato Fritters

500 g (1 lb) potatoes, peeled and grated

2 tablespoons plain flour

1 egg, beaten

1 onion, chopped

1 garlic clove, crushed

100 g (3½ oz) Emmental cheese, grated

sea salt and pepper

To garnish:

basil leaves

snipped chives

To serve:

griddled bacon

torn radicchio leaves

1. Place the grated potato on a clean tea towel, gather up the corners and twist into a tight ball to extract all the excess moisture from the potato. This is important otherwise the fritters will be soggy.
2. Mix together the flour and egg in a bowl until smooth. Add the potato and the remaining ingredients, season with sea salt and pepper and mix well.
3. Heat a griddle pan. Divide the mixture into 8 and place 4 portions of fritter mixture on the griddle. Flatten with a palette knife and cook for 4–5 minutes, then turn and cook for a further 4–5 minutes. Do not disturb the fritters while they are cooking as a crust needs to form on the cooking side, or they will be difficult to turn.
4. Keep the griddled fritters warm while you cook the remainder. Garnish with basil and snipped chives. Serve as an unusual side dish or with griddled bacon and radicchio as a starter.

Home-fried Potatoes

75 g (3 oz) butter or margarine
750 g (1½ lb) cooked potatoes, fairly
   thickly sliced
sea salt
chopped thyme, to garnish

1. Heat the butter or margarine in a
   large frying pan. Add the potatoes
   and sauté them gently for about
   10 minutes, turning them often until
   golden brown on both sides.
2. Sprinkle with sea salt and thyme just
   before serving.

Barbecued Potato Wedges with Sun-dried Tomato Aïoli

4 large potatoes, unpeeled

4 tablespoons olive oil

paprika, for sprinkling

coarse sea salt, for sprinkling

Sun-dried tomato aïoli:

4–6 garlic cloves, crushed

2 egg yolks

2 tablespoons lemon juice, plus extra to taste

300 ml (½ pint) extra virgin olive oil

8 sun-dried tomato halves in oil, drained and
   finely chopped

salt and pepper

1. If using wooden skewers, soak them in cold water for 30 minutes.
2. Cook the whole potatoes, in their skins, in a large saucepan of boiling water for about 20 minutes, or until just tender. Drain, and when cool enough to handle, cut each potato into large wedges.
3. To make the sun-dried tomato aïoli, place the garlic and egg yolks in a blender or food processor, add the lemon juice and mix briefly. With the motor running, gradually add the oil in a thin stream until the mixture forms a thick cream. Scrape into a bowl and stir in the sun-dried tomatoes. Season with salt and pepper and add extra lemon juice to taste, if necessary.
4. Brush the potato wedges with the olive oil, sprinkle with a little paprika and coarse sea salt and skewer or lay the potato wedges on a hot barbecue grill. Cook for 5–6 minutes, turning frequently, until golden brown all over. Serve with the aïoli.

Salmon and Potato Parcels

250 g (8 oz) potatoes, peeled

15 g (½ oz) butter

½ onion, finely chopped

¼ teaspoon fennel seeds, roughly ground

1 teaspoon finely grated lemon rind

1 tablespoon chopped dill

175 g (6 oz) smoked salmon, finely chopped

1 tablespoon lemon juice

1 egg yolk

500 g (1 lb) puff pastry, defrosted if frozen

salt and pepper

flour, for dusting

Egg glaze:

1 small egg

1 tablespoon milk

pinch of salt

1. Cook the potatoes in a large saucepan of lightly salted boiling water for about 20 minutes, or until tender.
2. Meanwhile, melt the butter in a small saucepan and fry the onion, fennel seeds and lemon rind for 10 minutes, until very soft. Transfer to a bowl.
3. Drain the cooked potatoes well and mash with a fork – the texture of the potato mash should remain fairly rough. Add to the onion in the bowl together with the dill, smoked salmon, lemon juice and egg yolk and mix until well blended. Season with salt and pepper.
4. Roll out the puff pastry on a lightly floured surface to form a thin rectangle, 17 x 34 cm (7 x 14 inches). Cut into 8 squares, measuring 8.5 cm (3½ inches).
5. Divide the filling among the squares, placing a mound of filling slightly off centre on each pastry square. Dampen the edges of the pastry and fold each one in half diagonally to form a triangle. Press the edges together to seal.
6. Transfer the pastry triangles to a lightly greased baking sheet. Beat together the ingredients for the egg glaze and brush the glaze lightly over the pastry. Bake in a preheated oven, 220°C (425°F), Gas Mark 7, for 15–20 minutes, until puffed up and golden. Serve hot.

Serves 4 / Preparation time: 25 minutes, plus salting and resting / Cooking time: 55–60 minutes / Oven temperature: 180°C (350°F), Gas Mark 4

Aubergine and Potato Bake

3 aubergines

5–6 tablespoons olive oil

2 onions, chopped

3 garlic cloves, crushed

4 large sun-ripened tomatoes, skinned, deseeded and chopped

2–3 sprigs of oregano or marjoram

2 large potatoes, cut into slices

sugar to taste (optional)

2 red peppers, cored, deseeded and sliced

salt and pepper

crusty bread, to serve

1. Quarter the aubergines lengthways, then halve each piece. Place in a colander, sprinkle evenly with salt and leave for 30 minutes–1 hour, to drain.

2. Make a tomato sauce by heating about 2 tablespoons of oil in a saucepan. Add the onions and garlic and fry gently until softened and lightly browned. Stir in the tomatoes, oregano or marjoram and simmer for about 15 minutes.

3. Meanwhile, heat a thin layer of oil in a large frying pan, add a single layer of potato slices and cook over a moderate heat until golden on both sides and about three-quarters cooked. Remove with a slotted spoon, drain on kitchen paper then place in a flameproof casserole. Repeat with the remaining potatoes.

4. Season the tomato sauce with salt and pepper, to taste, and add a little sugar, if necessary. Pour about one-third over the potatoes.

5. Rinse and pat dry the aubergine pieces, then fry in batches in the frying pan, adding more oil as necessary, until golden. Using a slotted spoon, transfer to kitchen paper to drain, then add to the casserole. Pour over another third of the tomato sauce.

6. Fry the red pepper slices in the pan, then add to the casserole. Pour over the remaining tomato sauce. Almost cover the casserole, leaving a small gap for steam to escape. Simmer very gently for 15–20 minutes, until the potatoes are tender and the sauce thick. Alternatively, bake, uncovered, in a preheated oven, 180°C (350°F), Gas Mark 4, for 15 minutes.

7. Let stand for 5–10 minutes before serving or cool to room temperature. Serve with plenty of crusty bread to mop up the juices.

Moroccan Potatoes with Harissa, Peppers and Tomatoes

3 tablespoons olive oil

750 g (1½ lb) potatoes, cut into chunks

1 large onion, sliced

2 red peppers, cored, deseeded and sliced

1 yellow pepper, cored, deseeded and sliced

4 well-flavoured tomatoes, cut into chunks

3 garlic cloves, crushed

3–4 teaspoons Harissa (see page 21)

salt

1. Heat 1 tablespoon of the oil in a large frying pan. Add the potatoes, stir to coat them in the oil, then cover the pan and fry over a low heat for 15 minutes, shaking the pan occasionally.
2. Add the remaining oil to the pan, then add the onion and red and yellow peppers. Increase the heat and cook, uncovered, for 10 minutes, stirring frequently, until the peppers have browned.
3. Add the tomatoes and garlic and continue to cook for about 4 minutes, until the tomatoes have softened. Add the harissa, season with salt and serve.

Potato Skins with Soured Cream Dip

5 large baking potatoes, scrubbed and dried
150 ml (¼ pint) soured cream
1 teaspoon snipped chives, plus extra to garnish
sunflower oil, for frying
salt and pepper

1. Prick the potatoes with a fork. Place directly on the shelf of a preheated oven, 200°C (400°F), Gas Mark 6, and bake for about 1¼ hours, or until soft.
2. Meanwhile, prepare the dip. Mix the soured cream in a bowl with the snipped chives. Season with salt and pepper, to taste. Cover the bowl and leave to chill.
3. When the potatoes are cooked, cool for a few minutes then cut each one into quarters lengthways. Scoop out most of the potato flesh, leaving a thin layer next to the skin. (Reserve the scooped-out potato for use in another recipe.)
4. Pour the oil into a small deep frying pan to a depth of 7.5 cm (3 inches). Heat the oil to 190°C (375°F), or until a cube of bread browns in 30 seconds. Carefully add a few potato skins to the hot oil and cook, in batches, for about 2 minutes, until brown and crisp. Remove and drain on kitchen paper.
5. To serve, arrange the potato skins on a plate with the dip, sprinkled with extra chives in the centre.

Beef and Potato Curry Puffs

625 g (1¼ lb) shortcrust pastry, defrosted
   if frozen
oil, for deep-frying
flour, for dusting

Filling:

1 tablespoon vegetable oil

1 small onion, finely chopped

2 garlic cloves, crushed

1 teaspoon grated fresh root ginger

1 small fresh red chilli, deseeded and
   finely chopped

2 tablespoons medium curry paste

250 g (8 oz) minced beef

½ teaspoon salt

175 g (6 oz) cooked potatoes, finely diced

1. Start by making the filling. Heat the vegetable oil in a heavy-based frying pan, add the onion, garlic, ginger and chilli and fry over a gentle heat, stirring constantly, for about 5 minutes, until softened. Stir in the curry paste and fry for about 1 minute, until fragrant.
2. Stir in the minced beef and salt, mix well and fry for 5 minutes, stirring occasionally. Stir in the diced potato and cook for a further 2 minutes. Taste and add more salt, if necessary, then leave the beef filling to cool.
3. Roll out the pastry thinly on a lightly floured surface. Using a pastry cutter, stamp out 24 x 10 cm (4 inch) circles and place 1 heaped teaspoon of beef filling on one half of each circle. Dampen the pastry edges with water and fold over each pastry circle to produce semi-circles. Press the edges together to seal.
4. Heat the oil for deep-frying in a saucepan. Deep-fry the curry puffs in batches, allowing 5–6 minutes for each batch and turning halfway through cooking, until they are crisp and golden. (Do not allow the oil to get too hot or the pastry will burn.)
5. Remove the puffs from the pan with a slotted spoon and drain on kitchen paper. Leave to cool slightly and serve warm or cold, as liked.

Serves 4 / Preparation time: 10 minutes, plus cooling / Cooking time: 30–35 minutes / Oven temperature: 200°C (400°F), Gas Mark 6

Potatoes Wrapped in Parma Ham

12 small new potatoes scrubbed but
   unpeeled

12 very thin slices of Parma ham

2 tablespoons olive oil

sea salt

1. Cook the potatoes in a large saucepan of boiling water for 10–15 minutes, or until tender. Drain well and allow to go cold.
2. Roll each cooked potato in a slice of Parma ham, patting with your hands to mould the ham to the shape of the potato.
3. Brush a roasting tin with the oil. Add the ham-wrapped potatoes and cook in a preheated oven, 200°C (400°F), Gas Mark 6, for 20 minutes. Keep an eye on the potatoes while they are cooking as they may need turning, or moving around – often the ones on the edge get more colour than the ones in the middle.
4. Serve the potatoes sprinkled with sea salt.

FOOD FACT Parma ham is a good-quality, dry-cured, raw ham from Italy. It is lightly salted and probably best recognized as the transparently thin slices often served with fresh melon or figs as a starter.

Rösti

With its crisp golden crust and soft stringy centre, this Swiss potato pancake is very easy to make. The dish originated as a way of using up leftover cooked potatoes. The secret of a good rösti is to grate the potatoes when cold, which keeps the grated potato strands separate. Serve with grilled sausages, liver and onions, or baked fish, or serve it topped with a fried egg or with a tomato sauce.

**1 kg (2 lb) even-sized floury potatoes, scrubbed
   but unpeeled**
75 g (3 oz) butter
1 small mild onion, very finely chopped
salt and pepper

1. Cook the potatoes in a large saucepan of lightly salted boiling water for about 7 minutes. Drain well. When the potatoes are quite cold, peel them and grate them coarsely into a bowl.
2. Heat 15 g (½ oz) of the butter in a large, heavy-based frying pan. Add the onion and cook for about 5 minutes, until soft. Stir into the grated potato and season with salt and pepper, to taste.
3. Melt the remaining butter in the frying pan. Set aside about 1 tablespoon of the melted butter in a cup. Add the potato mixture to the pan and form into a neat cake. Cook gently for about 15 minutes, or until the underside of the cake is a crusty golden brown, shaking the pan occasionally so that the rösti cake does not stick.
4. To cook the top of the rösti, pour over the reserved melted butter and either place the frying pan under a preheated grill to brown, or turn the rösti over in the pan and brown.
5. To serve, invert the rösti cake on to a warmed flat dish and cut it into wedges.

**Serves 4 / Preparation time: 5 minutes / Cooking time: 35–40 minutes /
Oven temperature: 220°C (425°F), Gas Mark 7**

Roasted Paprika Potato Wedges

4 large baking potatoes, about
   250 g (8 oz) each, left unpeeled
4 tablespoons olive or sunflower oil
1–2 teaspoons paprika
salt
soured cream mixed with chives or
   Aïoli (see page 21) or
   mayonnaise, to serve

1. Scrub the potatoes well, rinse under cold running water and pat dry with a tea towel. Cut each potato lengthways into 8 wedges.
2. Place the potato wedges in a roasting tin, drizzle over the oil and toss well to coat. Sprinkle over the paprika and season with salt. Place the potatoes in the top of a preheated oven, 220°C (425°F), Gas Mark 7, and roast for 35–40 minutes, basting with the oil 2–3 times during cooking, until they are tender and nicely browned.
3. Serve the wedges as a starter with a bowl of soured cream mixed with snipped chives, or with aïoli or mayonnaise, or as a side dish to replace traditional roast potatoes or chips.

Serves 4 / Preparation time: 10–15 minutes / Cooking time: about 30 minutes

Griddled Warm New Potatoes with Fresh Mint Dressing

This makes a wonderful, fresh-tasting accompaniment to lamb chops.

750 g (1½ lb) small new potatoes, scrubbed
and halved lengthways
mint leaves, to garnish

Dressing:
finely grated rind and juice of 2 limes
8 tablespoons grapeseed oil
2 tablespoons chopped mint
coarse sea salt and pepper

1. Place a layer of potato slices on a preheated hot griddle and cook for 6 minutes on each side, reducing the heat as required. Remove and keep warm while cooking the remaining potato slices.

2. Combine the lime rind and juice and the oil in a small jug, beating well with a whisk. Add sea salt and pepper and chopped mint and whisk until evenly combined. Alternatively, place all the dressing ingredients in a screw-top jar and shake well to combine thoroughly.

3. Toss the cooked potatoes in the dressing, pile into a serving dish and serve garnished with mint leaves.

Serves 4 / Preparation time: 5 minutes, plus soaking / Cooking time: 10–15 minutes

Perfect French Fries

4 potatoes, peeled
sunflower oil, for deep-frying
sea salt

1. Thinly slice the potatoes crossways, using a sharp knife, a mandolin or the slicing blade of a food processor. Soak the slices in ice-cold water for 15–20 minutes to remove the excess starch and to crisp the potatoes.
2. Drain the potato slices and dry them thoroughly on a clean tea towel or kitchen paper.
3. Heat the oil for deep-frying to 190°C (375°F), or until a cube of bread browns in about 30 seconds. Place a few potato slices in the frying basket and lower it into the oil. Cook for 3–5 minutes, until the chips are golden brown, turning if necessary. Remove the basket and drain the fries on kitchen paper. Repeat with the remaining potato slices.
4. Serve the fries, sprinkled with sea salt.

**Serves 6 / Preparation time: 25 minutes / Cooking time: 45 minutes /
Oven temperature: 200°C (400°F), Gas Mark 6**

Parsnip Duchesse Potatoes

750 g (1½ lb) parsnips, peeled and cut into
　even-sized pieces
750 g (1½ lb) potatoes, peeled and cut into
　even-sized pieces
pinch of ground nutmeg
1 egg, beaten
salt and pepper

1. Cook the parsnips and potatoes separately in large saucepans of lightly salted boiling water for about 20 minutes, or until tender.
2. Drain the vegetables well, then mash together using a potato masher or fork. Beat until smooth, then rub through a sieve. Turn the purée into a bowl, season well with salt and pepper and beat in the nutmeg and egg.
3. Spoon the vegetable mixture into a piping bag fitted with a large star nozzle and pipe large whirls of the mixture on to a greased baking sheet.
4. Bake in a preheated oven, 200°C (400°F), Gas Mark 6, for about 25 minutes, until lightly browned. Serve hot.

Serves 4 / Preparation time: 15 minutes / Cooking time: 1–1½ hours /
Oven temperature: 220°C (425°F), Gas Mark 7, then 180°C (350°F), Gas Mark 4

Baked Cheese Soufflé Potatoes

4 baking potatoes, scrubbed

125 g (4 oz) Gruyère cheese, grated

freshly grated nutmeg

125 g (4 oz) butter

4 tablespoons double cream

2 eggs, separated

salt and pepper

1. Prick the potatoes with a fork. Place directly on the shelf of a preheated oven, 220°C (425°F), Gas Mark 7, and bake for about 1 hour, or until the potatoes feel soft. Remove the potatoes from the oven and lower the oven temperature to 180°C (350°F), Gas Mark 4.
2. Using a sharp kitchen knife, slice each potato in half lengthways. Scoop the soft potato flesh into a mixing bowl. Arrange the potato shells on a baking sheet and return to the oven to crisp them.
3. Mash the scooped-out potato with a fork. Mix in the grated cheese, a seasoning of salt and pepper and a grating of nutmeg. Add the butter, cream and egg yolks to the potato mixture and beat with a wooden spoon, until smooth and soft.
4. Place the egg whites in a clean bowl and whisk them into stiff peaks. Fold them carefully into the potato mixture with a metal tablespoon. Pile the mixture back into the potato skins and return to the oven for 20–25 minutes, or until golden, before serving.

Makes 8 / Preparation time: 20 minutes / Cooking time: 30–35 minutes

Makes 10–12 / Preparation time: 15 minutes / Cooking time: 30 minutes

Boxty Pancakes

Sometimes referred to as 'stamp', this is a traditional Irish potato dish, found in the northern counties of Cavan, Donegal, Leitrim and Monaghan.

2 tablespoons plain flour

1 teaspoon baking powder

500 g (1 lb) potatoes, peeled and coarsely
   grated

150 ml (¼ pint) milk

oil, for frying

salt and pepper

butter, jam or fried bacon, to serve

1. Sift the flour into a bowl with the baking powder.

2. Place the grated potatoes in another bowl and add the sifted flour. Season with salt and pepper and stir in the milk.

3. Drop tablespoons of this mixture on to a hot, lightly oiled frying pan or griddle. Cook for about 5 minutes on each side, until golden brown. Serve hot, with butter and jam or with fried bacon.

Makes a 500 g (1 lb) loaf / Preparation time: 15 minutes, plus rising / Cooking time: 30 minutes
Oven temperature: 200°C (400°F), Gas Mark 6, then 180°C (350°F), Gas Mark 5

Roquefort Bread

500 g (1 lb) strong white flour, plus extra,
  for dusting
2 teaspoons salt
25 g (1 oz) butter, plus extra, for greasing
7 g (¼ oz) sachet fast-action dried yeast
150 ml (¼ pint) lukewarm milk
250 g (8 oz) cooked potato, sieved
125 g (4 oz) Roquefort or other blue cheese,
  crumbled
beaten egg, to glaze

1. Sift the flour with the salt into a warmed bowl. Rub in the butter until the mixture resembles fine breadcrumbs. Stir in the yeast. Stir the milk into the sieved potato in another bowl, then work this mixture into the flour to make a soft but not sticky dough. Knead on a lightly floured surface for 5 minutes, then knead in the crumbled cheese.

2. Grease a 500 g (1 lb) loaf tin. Shape the dough to fit the tin, or shape into a round cob shape and place on a greased baking sheet. Cover with waxed paper and leave to rise in a warm place for 30 minutes, or until the loaf has doubled in size.

3. Brush the loaf with beaten egg and bake in a preheated oven, 200°C (400°F), Gas Mark 6, for 15 minutes. Lower the heat to 180°C (350°F), Gas Mark 4, and bake for a further 15 minutes. Turn the loaf out of the tin, if using, and leave to cool on a wire rack.

Makes 6 / Preparation time: 5–10 minutes, plus cooking and mashing potatoes / Cooking time: 5 minutes

Potato Bread

This Irish potato bread is cooked on a cast-iron griddle or in a heavy-based frying pan, which is heated gently without fat or oil, only a light dusting of flour before using.

250 g (8 oz) warm, cooked and mashed potatoes
½ teaspoon salt
25 g (1 oz) butter, melted
50 g (2 oz) plain flour, plus extra for dusting.

1. Place the potatoes in a large bowl and mix in the salt and melted butter. Stir in the flour to make a pliable dough. Turn on to a lightly floured surface and roll into a round, about 5 mm (¼ inch) thick and 23 cm (9 inches) in diameter. Cut into 6 triangular shapes (called farls).
2. Lightly dust a cast-iron griddle or heavy-based frying pan with flour and heat the pan. When the flour begins to turn a pale beige colour, the temperature is right for cooking. Arrange the farls on the pan and cook for about 2½ minutes on each side, until lightly browned.
3. Serve them hot with butter and sugar or homemade jam. Alternatively, the cooked bread may be fried and eaten with bacon, sausages and egg as part of a traditional cooked breakfast.

TIP Potato bread is best made while the potatoes are still hot. If using leftovers, heat for 30 seconds in a microwave oven before mixing with the rest of the ingredients. Instead of making farls, you could cut the potato bread into 10 circles, using a 7 cm (3 inch) plain cutter.

Serves 4 / Preparation time: 10 minutes / Cooking time: 35 minutes / Oven temperature: 230°C (450°F), Gas Mark 8

Potato Bravas

1 kg (2 lb) small potatoes, unpeeled
2 tablespoons olive oil
sea salt

Sauce:

4 tablespoons olive oil
2 tablespoons water
1 tablespoon tomato purée
1 tablespoon red wine vinegar
1 teaspoon chilli sauce
2 teaspoons paprika
salt and pepper

1. Cut the potatoes into 1 cm (½ inch) thick slices and place in a single layer on a baking sheet.
2. Brush with olive oil, sprinkle with sea salt and cook in a preheated oven, 230°C (450°F), Gas Mark 8, for 20 minutes. Turn the potatoes over and bake for a further 10 minutes, until crisp.
3. Meanwhile, combine all the sauce ingredients in a sauté pan. Add the cooked potatoes and heat through. Season with salt and pepper to taste and serve hot.

5 Main Meals

Gnocchi:

1 kg (2 lb) floury potatoes, unpeeled

1 teaspoon salt

50 g (2 oz) butter

1 egg, beaten

250–300 g (8–10 oz) plain white flour

plain white or semolina flour, for sprinkling

Pesto sauce:

50 g (2 oz) basil leaves, roughly chopped

25 g (1 oz) pine nuts, roughly chopped

2 garlic cloves

4 tablespoons olive oil

juice of ½ lemon

40 g (1½ oz) Parmesan cheese, freshly grated

salt and pepper

To serve:

3 tablespoons butter, plus extra, for greasing

freshly grated Parmesan cheese

Gnocchi with Pesto

If made properly, these dumplings from northern Italy will be as light as a feather. The secret is to use floury potatoes, cook them in their skins and mix the dough while still warm. A light hand is needed, and as little flour as possible.

1. Cook the potatoes in a large saucepan of boiling water for 20–30 minutes, or until they are very tender.

2. Meanwhile, make the pesto sauce. Put the basil and pine nuts in a mortar with the garlic, and season with salt and pepper. Pound together until reduced to a thick paste. Transfer to a bowl and add the oil, a little at a time, stirring constantly, until thick. Stir in the lemon juice and grated Parmesan. Cover and set aside.

3. Drain the cooked potatoes well. Holding the warm potatoes in a tea towel, peel and pass them through a potato ricer or sieve into a bowl.

4. While the potatoes are still warm, add the salt, butter, beaten egg and half of the plain flour. Lightly mix together, then turn out on to a lightly floured surface. Gradually knead the rest of the flour into the dough until it is smooth, soft and a little sticky.

5. Roll the dough into long 'sausages', about 2.5 cm (1 inch) thick, and cut them into 1.5 cm (¾ inch) pieces. Take each piece and roll it over the back of a fork with your floured thumb so that the gnocchi have ridges on one side and an indentation on the other. Spread the gnocchi out on a tea towel sprinkled with plain white or semolina flour.

6. Cook the gnocchi, a few at a time, in a large saucepan of lightly salted, gently boiling water for 2–3 minutes, or until they rise to the surface. Remove from the pan with a slotted spoon and place in a buttered serving dish. Dot with the butter and pour the pesto sauce over the top. Serve immediately, sprinkled with grated Parmesan.

FOOD FACT   Pesto is a sauce originating from Genoa in Italy. The main ingredients are garlic, pine nuts, fresh basil and grated Parmesan, which are pounded together to make a thick creamy paste. Commercial bottled versions are available, but do not compare with home-made pesto, which is redolent with fresh basil and can easily be made in a food processor.

Carnival Chicken with Sweet Potato Mash

4 skinless chicken breasts, about 150 g
  (5 oz) each
sprigs of flat leaf parsley, to garnish

Marinade:

100 ml (3½ fl oz) sweet sherry
1 teaspoon Angostura bitters
1 tablespoon light soy sauce
1 tablespoon chopped fresh root ginger
pinch of ground cumin
pinch of ground coriander
1 teaspoon dried mixed herbs
1 small onion, finely chopped
75 ml (3 fl oz) fresh chicken stock

Sweet potato mash:

2 sweet potatoes, unpeeled
2 tablespoons low-fat fromage frais (optional)
salt and pepper

1. Place the chicken breasts in a nonmetallic dish. Mix all the marinade ingredients together in a bowl. Spoon over the chicken, making sure the pieces are well coated. Cover and leave to marinate in the refrigerator overnight.

2. When you are ready to cook, place the marinated chicken on a grill pan and cook under a preheated medium grill for 20 minutes, turning over halfway through cooking.

3. Meanwhile, cook the sweet potatoes in their skins in a large saucepan of boiling water for 20 minutes, until soft. Drain well then, holding the warm potatoes in a tea towel, peel them carefully. Mash the potato using a potato masher or fork and let it dry off a bit before stirring in the fromage frais, if using. Season with salt and pepper, to taste, and serve with the chicken. Garnish with the flat leaf parsley.

Serves 4 / Preparation time: 35 minutes, plus infusing and cooling / Cooking time: 40 minutes / Oven temperature: 200°C (400°F), Gas Mark 6

250 g (8 oz) frozen or fresh mixed vegetables, diced

butter, for frying

125 g (4 oz) mushrooms, sliced

1 large or 2 medium onions, thinly sliced

75 g (3 oz) Cheddar cheese, grated

1 egg yolk, beaten

salt and pepper

Potato pastry:

250 g (8 oz) self-raising flour

175 g (6 oz) butter or soft margarine

1 teaspoon salt

250 g (8 oz) cold, cooked mashed potato

1 tablespoon milk

Béchamel sauce:

150 ml (¼ pint) milk

½ small onion, roughly chopped

1 bay leaf

15 g (½ oz) butter

15 g (1/2 oz) plain flour

Vegetable Pie with Potato Pastry

1. Begin by infusing the milk for the béchamel sauce. Put the milk, onion and bay leaf in a small saucepan. Heat gently until just boiling. Remove the pan from the heat and set aside for 20 minutes to allow the flavours to infuse.
2. To make the potato pastry, place the flour in a bowl, add the butter or margarine and rub in using your fingertips. Mix in the salt and work the mashed potato into the mixture, adding the 1 tablespoon of milk a little at a time.
3. Turn the dough on to a lightly floured surface and knead until smooth and fairly soft. Roll out and use it to line a large shallow ovenproof dish. Bake blind (see Tip) in a preheated oven, 200°C (400°F), Gas Mark 6, for 15 minutes, or until the pie case is light golden brown.
4. Meanwhile, continue with the béchamel sauce. Strain the infused milk and set aside. Melt the butter for the sauce in the pan, stir in the flour and cook over a gentle heat for 1 minute. Remove from the heat and gradually beat in the infused milk, a little at a time, until evenly blended. Return to a low heat and stir constantly until the sauce thickens. Bring the sauce to a gentle boil, still stirring, and simmer for 2 minutes, then remove from the heat and set aside to cool.
5. To make the filling, cook the diced mixed vegetables in a saucepan of lightly salted boiling water, until just tender. Drain and leave to cool. Heat a little butter in a small pan and fry the mushrooms lightly, then remove and leave to cool. Add the onions to the pan and fry lightly, then leave to cool.
6. Stir all the cooked vegetables into the béchamel sauce and season with salt and pepper, to taste.
7. Remove the pastry case from the oven, allow to cool a little then remove the lining paper and fill with the vegetable mixture, spreading with a palette knife so that it is smooth and flat. Sprinkle with the grated Cheddar. Brush the edges of the pastry with the beaten egg yolk and return to the oven for 15 minutes, or until the cheese has melted and is beginning to brown. Serve hot.

TIP Baking blind means precooking a pastry base without a filling. After lining the dish with the pastry, prick it all over with a fork. Cut a piece of greaseproof paper to the shape of the dish and about 5 cm (2 inches) larger all round, and place it over the pastry. Pour enough dried beans over the paper to cover it, then place in the oven for 15 minutes, as directed.

Griddled Sausage with Mustard Mash

8 speciality sausages
2 onions, cut into wedges, roots left intact

Mustard mash:
1 kg (2 lb) potatoes, quartered but unpeeled
75 g (3 oz) butter
1 tablespoon wholegrain mustard
3 teaspoons prepared English mustard
1 garlic clove, crushed
1 large bunch of parsley, chopped
dash of olive oil
salt and pepper

1. First make the mustard mash. Cook the potatoes in a large saucepan of boiling water for about 20 minutes, or until tender.
2. Place the sausages on a preheated griddle and cook for 10 minutes, turning them to get an even colour. Add the onion wedges and cook for 6–7 minutes with the sausages.
3. Meanwhile, drain the cooked potatoes well and return them to the pan. Place over a low heat and allow any excess water to steam away, without colouring the potatoes. Remove from the heat then, holding the warm potatoes in a tea towel, peel them carefully and mash well, using a potato masher or fork. Add the butter, wholegrain and English mustards, garlic and salt and pepper, and continue to mash. Taste the potato and add more mustard, if liked. Finally, stir in the parsley and a dash of olive oil.
4. Serve the mash and sausages together with the griddled onion wedges.

Lamb Shanks with Olives and Sun-dried Tomatoes with Creamy Saffron Mash

2 tablespoons plain flour

4 lamb shanks, about 500 g (1 lb) each

2 tablespoons olive oil

2 red onions, sliced

2 tablespoons rosemary leaves

3 garlic cloves, chopped

100 ml (3½ fl oz) balsamic vinegar

200 ml (7 fl oz) red wine

50 g (2 oz) pitted black olives, quartered

40 g (1½ oz) sun-dried tomatoes, cut into
    strips lengthways

175 ml (6 fl oz) water

salt and pepper

Creamy saffron mash:

1 kg (2 lb) potatoes, peeled and cut into
    large chunks

125 ml (4 fl oz) single cream

large pinch of saffron threads

5 tablespoons extra virgin olive oil

salt and pepper

1. Season the flour with a little salt and pepper and toss the lamb in the flour, shaking off any excess.

2. Heat the oil in a large flameproof casserole – large enough to accommodate the lamb shanks in one layer. Add the lamb and brown well all over. Remove with a slotted spoon and set aside.

3. Lower the heat, add the onions and cook for about 10 minutes, until softened. Add the rosemary and garlic and cook for a further 2–3 minutes. Increase the heat, add the balsamic vinegar and red wine and boil rapidly until reduced by half. Stir in the olives, sun-dried tomatoes and water.

4. Lower the heat again and place the lamb shanks on top of the sauce, cover with a tight-fitting lid and cook for 1½–2 hours, until very tender. Alternatively, cook in a preheated oven, 200°C (400°F), Gas Mark 6. Check occasionally, basting the lamb shanks and adding more water, if necessary.

5. Meanwhile, make the saffron mash. Cook the potatoes in a large saucepan of boiling water for about 20 minutes, until just tender. Heat the single cream to simmering point in a small saucepan, remove from the heat and stir in the saffron threads. Leave to infuse for 10 minutes.

6. When the potatoes are cooked, drain well, return to the dry pan and add the saffron cream and oil. Mash together well using a potato masher or fork and season with salt and pepper to taste.

7. To serve, place a spoonful of the saffron mash on each plate, top with a lamb shank and spoon some sauce over the top.

Chargrilled Poussins with Sweet Potatoes and Red Lentils

4 poussins, spatchcocked (see page 20) about 500 g (1 lb) each

4 tablespoons sunflower oil

50 g (2 oz) shallots, grated

2 garlic cloves, crushed

50 g (2 oz) carrot, grated

200 g (7 oz) red lentils

200 ml (7 fl oz) chicken stock

4 teaspoons Thai red curry paste

300 g (10 oz) sweet potatoes, peeled and diced

1 teaspoon cumin seeds

small handful of coriander leaves, chopped

salt and pepper

Marinade:

4 tablespoons Dijon mustard

6 garlic cloves, crushed

125 ml (4 fl oz) sunflower oil

few sprigs of rosemary

To garnish:

olive oil, for drizzling

1 lemon, quartered

sprigs of rosemary

1. To make the marinade, put the Dijon mustard and garlic into a blender or food processor. Blend the ingredients together then, with the motor running, slowly pour in the sunflower oil to form a smooth paste. Transfer the paste to a large shallow dish and add the rosemary.

2. Turn the spatchcocked poussins in the mustard mixture and coat them well. Cover and leave to marinate in the refrigerator for 24 hours.

3. Heat 2 tablespoons of the oil in a large saucepan, add the shallots, garlic, carrot and lentils and turn in the oil. Add half the stock and bring to the boil. Lower the heat and simmer gently, adding more stock, a ladleful at a time, until all the stock has been used and the lentils are cooked. Stir in the curry paste and season with salt and pepper to taste. Cover and set aside.

4. Heat the remaining oil in another saucepan, add the sweet potatoes and cumin seeds and fry for 7–10 minutes, until the sweet potatoes are soft but not browned.

5. Remove the poussins from the marinade and cook under a preheated hot grill or on a barbecue for 10 minutes on each side, or until tender and cooked right through.

6. Meanwhile, gently reheat the lentil mixture and stir in the sweet potatoes and coriander. To serve, divide the lentil and sweet potato mixture between 4 warmed plates. Place the poussins on top and drizzle with a little olive oil. Garnish with the lemon quarters and sprigs of rosemary and serve hot.

Massaman Potato Curry

750 ml (1¼ pints) coconut milk

400 g (13 oz) potatoes, peeled and cut into
even-sized pieces

50 g (2 oz) roasted peanuts, crushed

1 large onion, chopped

5 tablespoons tamarind water

75 g (3 oz) palm or soft brown sugar

2 teaspoons salt

basil leaves, to garnish

Massaman curry paste:

3 cardamom pods

1 teaspoon coriander seeds

1 teaspoon cumin seeds

2 cloves

6 small fresh red chillies

2 garlic cloves, halved

1 teaspoon ground cinnamon

1 cm (½ inch) piece of fresh root ginger, peeled
and finely chopped

3 shallots, chopped

1 lemon grass stalk, chopped

juice of ½ lime

To serve:

naan bread or rice

salad

1. First make the curry paste. Remove the seeds from the cardamom pods and dry-fry the cardamom seeds in a small frying pan for 2 minutes with the coriander and cumin seeds and the cloves. Transfer the dry-fried spices to a blender or food processor and blend with the remaining curry paste ingredients to make a thick paste. Alternatively, use a pestle and mortar.

2. Heat the coconut milk in a large saucepan and add 2 tablespoons of the curry paste, or to taste. Stir to blend, then heat until simmering. (Transfer any remaining curry paste to an airtight container and store in the refrigerator for up to 3 weeks.)

3. Lower the heat, add the potatoes to the pan and cook for 6 minutes.

4. Add the crushed roasted peanuts, onion, tamarind water, sugar and salt. Stir thoroughly to dissolve the sugar and continue to simmer, stirring, for 5 minutes.

5. Increase the heat and allow the liquid to bubble until the potato is tender. Garnish with basil leaves before serving with naan bread or rice and a salad.

Serves 4 / Preparation time: 30–35 minutes, plus chilling / Cooking time: 25 minutes

Salmon Fish Cakes

300 g (10 oz) potatoes, left unpeeled

25 g (1 oz) butter or margarine

300 g (10 oz) fresh salmon, cooked and flaked

2 tablespoons chopped parsley

2 eggs, beaten

75 g (3 oz) dry natural breadcrumbs

flour, for dusting

oil, for frying

salt and pepper

chives, to garnish

tomato salad, to serve

1. Cook the potatoes in a large saucepan of boiling water for about 20 minutes, or until tender. Drain well then, holding the warm potatoes in a tea towel, peel them carefully.
2. Using a potato masher or fork, mash the potatoes in a bowl with the butter or margarine, then mix in the flaked salmon, parsley, salt and pepper to taste and half of the beaten egg. Cover and chill for 20 minutes.
3. Place the salmon and potato mixture on a lightly floured surface and shape into a roll. Cut into 8 slices and shape each one into a flat round, about 6 cm (2½ inches) in diameter. Dip the rounds into the remaining beaten egg, then coat with breadcrumbs.
4. Heat the oil in a frying pan, add the fish cakes, in batches, and fry for 2–3 minutes on each side, or until golden brown and heated through. Garnish with chives and serve with a tomato salad.

Venison Stew with Parsnip and Potato Champ

1–2 tablespoons oil

1 onion, finely chopped

750 g–1 kg (1½–2 lb) lean, boneless venison, cut into 2.5 cm (1 inch) cubes

25 g (1 oz) plain flour

300 ml (½ pint) Guinness

750 ml (1¼ pints) game stock or water

1 bay leaf

1 sprig of marjoram

12–18 pickling onions, peeled

125–175 g (4–6 oz) celery, cut into 2.5 cm (1 inch) lengths

2 tablespoons finely chopped parsley

salt and pepper

Parsnip and potato champ:

500–750 g (1–1½ lb) potatoes, peeled and cut into even-sized pieces

500–750 g (1–1½ lb) parsnips, peeled and cut into even-sized pieces

butter, for mashing

salt and pepper

1. Heat half the oil in a large frying pan and fry the onion until soft and beginning to brown. Transfer the onion to a large flameproof casserole.
2. Heat the remaining oil in the pan and fry the meat, a little at a time, until brown. Add to the onion. Stir in the flour and add the Guinness and stock, together with the bay leaf and marjoram and season with salt and pepper.
3. Bring to the boil, then lower the heat and simmer gently for 1–1½ hours, until the meat is almost tender. (Alternatively, cook the stew in a preheated oven, 150–160°C (300–325°F), Gas Mark 2–3, for the same length of time.) Add the onions and celery 15–30 minutes before the end of the cooking time.
4. Start making the parsnip and potato champ about 30 minutes before the stew will be ready. Cook the potatoes and parsnips separately in large saucepans of boiling water for about 20 minutes, or until tender. Drain and dry well, then mash together with plenty of butter and salt and pepper to taste, using a potato masher or fork.
5. To serve, taste the stew and adjust the seasoning, if necessary. Stir in the finely chopped parsley and serve with the parsnip and potato champ.

Serves 4 / Preparation time: 20 minutes / Cooking time: 40–45 minutes / Oven temperature: 200°C (400°F), Gas Mark 6

Potato Tart with Ham, Artichokes and Mushrooms

Potato dough:

75 g (3 oz) butter, plus extra for greasing

1 onion, thinly sliced

150 g (5 oz) plain flour

125 g (4 oz) cold, cooked mashed potato

salt and pepper

Topping:

1 tablespoon olive oil

2 shallots, sliced

125 g (4 oz) mushrooms, sliced

125 g (4 oz) cooked ham, cut into strips

175 g (6 oz) drained canned artichoke
   hearts, sliced

salt and pepper

This free-form tart has a moist, scone-like dough, which is perfect for all sorts of savoury toppings.

1. To make the dough, melt 25 g (1 oz) of the butter in a small saucepan. Add the onion and fry for about 5 minutes, until softened and lightly browned. Cool slightly.

2. Place the flour in a mixing bowl. Dice the remaining butter and rub it into the flour. Add the onion with the pan juices, the mashed potato, and salt and pepper, to taste. Mix to a soft dough.

3. Press out the dough on a greased baking sheet to a 23 cm (9 inch) round. Pinch the edges of the dough upwards to make a slight rim.

4. To make the topping, heat the oil in a frying pan, add the shallots and fry until lightly browned. Add the mushrooms and cook briefly, until softened.

5. Scatter the ham and artichoke hearts over the dough, then top with the shallot and mushroom mixture. Season with salt and pepper and bake in a preheated oven, 200°C (400°F), Gas Mark 6, for 25–30 minutes, until the pastry is golden brown. Serve hot.

FOOD FACT The globe artichoke is the flower head of a type of thistle, probably native to North Africa but now cultivated in Europe and North America. Some of the artichoke's flavour lies in the fat base of each of its leaves, but the best part is its tender base, or heart, deep within the centre of the vegetable. Artichoke hearts are available bottled in oil, canned or frozen.

**Serves 6 / Preparation time: 40 minutes, plus cooling / Cooking time: 1¾ hours /
Oven temperature: 190°C (375°F), Gas Mark 5**

Chicken and Mushroom Pie

1.5 kg (3 lb) chicken with giblets

1 bouquet garni

1 small onion, quartered

6–8 black peppercorns

25 g (1 oz) butter

2 leeks, trimmed, cleaned and thinly sliced

125 g (4 oz) button mushrooms, sliced

1 teaspoon plain flour

125 g (4 oz) full-fat soft cheese

2 tablespoons chopped parsley

salt

sprigs of parsley, to garnish

Topping:

500 g (1 lb) potatoes, peeled and cut into
    even-sized pieces

250 g (8 oz) carrots, sliced

25 g (1 oz) butter

1 egg, beaten

pinch of ground nutmeg

salt and pepper

1. Put the chicken and giblets into a large saucepan with the bouquet garni, onion, black peppercorns and a little salt. Cover with water, bring to the boil, then skim the surface. Cover the pan and simmer for about 1 hour, or until the chicken is cooked. To test, pierce the thickest part of the leg with a fine skewer – the juices should run clear.

2. Remove the chicken and set aside. When it is cool enough to handle, skin it and cut the meat from the bones. Place the chicken pieces in an ovenproof dish and set aside. (Reserve the chicken stock for use in another recipe or for making soup.)

3. Melt the butter in a small pan and fry the leeks and mushrooms over a moderate heat for 3 minutes, stirring. Stir in the flour, then the soft cheese and chopped parsley. Simmer for 3 minutes, then spread the vegetables over the pieces of chicken.

4. To make the topping, cook the potatoes and carrots separately in large saucepans of lightly salted boiling water for about 20 minutes, or until tender. Drain well then mash them together using a potato masher or fork and beat in the butter and egg. Season to taste with nutmeg, salt and pepper.

5. Spread the potato and carrot topping evenly over the chicken and vegetables, then fork it up into peaks.

6. Bake in a preheated oven, 190°C (375°F), Gas Mark 5, for 20–25 minutes, until the topping is well browned. Garnish with sprigs of parsley and serve hot.

Serves 4 / Preparation time: 20 minutes, plus chilling / Cooking time: 20–25 minutes

Crab Cakes

50 g (2 oz) butter or margarine

1 onion, finely chopped

50 g (2 oz) mushrooms, chopped

50 g (2 oz) plain flour

150 ml (¼ pint) milk

1 teaspoon Worcestershire sauce

2 tablespoons chopped parsley

250 g (8 oz) fresh, canned or frozen
  cooked crabmeat

250 g (8 oz) cooked floury potatoes, mashed
  without any additional liquid

2 eggs, beaten

75 g (3 oz) dry natural breadcrumbs

4 tablespoons sunflower oil or 50 g (2 oz) butter

salt and pepper

1. Heat the butter or margarine in a saucepan. Add the onion and mushrooms and cook gently until soft. Add half of the flour and stir over a low heat for 2–3 minutes.
2. Blend in the milk and stir as the liquid comes to a boil and thickens. Season lightly and add the Worcestershire sauce, parsley and crabmeat.
3. Blend the mashed potatoes with the crabmeat mixture. Chill until firm enough to form into 8 round cakes.
4. Season the remaining flour and use to coat the crab cakes all over. Brush them with beaten egg, then roll in the dry breadcrumbs.
5. Heat the sunflower oil or butter in a large frying pan and cook the crabcakes, in batches, until crisp and brown on both sices.

Baked Cod with Potatoes and Olives

375 g (12 oz) potatoes, peeled and thinly sliced
sprig of thyme, separated into leaves
4 cod fillets, about 200 g (7 oz) each
2 tablespoons pitted black olives
2 tablespoons olive oil
butter, for greasing
salt and pepper

1. Arrange the potatoes in layers in a well-buttered shallow ovenproof dish, sprinkling each layer with a little thyme and salt and pepper.
2. Place the pieces of cod on top of the potatoes, add the olives and drizzle with olive oil. Season with salt and pepper and add a little more thyme.
3. Place the dish in the middle of a preheated oven, 220°C (425°F), Gas Mark 7, and cook for 25 minutes. Check that the potatoes are soft before serving.

Sweet Potato and Spinach Curry

1. Cook the sweet potato chunks in a large saucepan of lightly salted boiling water for 8–10 minutes, or until tender. Drain well and set aside.

2. Heat the oil in a saucepan, add the onion, garlic, shrimp paste and turmeric and fry over a gentle heat, stirring frequently, for 3 minutes. Stir in the chilli and fry for a further 2 minutes.

3. Add the coconut milk, stir to mix, then simmer for 3–4 minutes, until the coconut milk has thickened slightly. Stir in the cooked sweet potatoes and some salt to taste, then cook the curry for 4 minutes.

4. Stir in the spinach, cover the pan and simmer gently for 2–3 minutes, or until the spinach has wilted and the curry has heated through. Taste and adjust the seasoning, if necessary then serve the curry immediately with naan bread or chapatis, if liked.

500 g (1 lb) sweet potatoes, peeled and cut into large chunks

3 tablespoons groundnut oil

1 red onion, chopped

2 garlic cloves, crushed

1 teaspoon shrimp paste

1 teaspoon ground turmeric

1 large fresh red chilli, deseeded and chopped

400 ml (14 fl oz) coconut milk

250 g (8 oz) ready-washed young leaf spinach

salt

naan bread or chapatis, to serve (optional)

FOOD FACT Spinach is one of the most widely grown and popular of the leafy vegetables. It has a subtle, faintly bitter-sweet taste and its leaves may be small and rounded or larger and more pointed, curly or smooth. Spinach needs thorough washing to remove the grit often found within it. It is at its best eaten raw in salads or only lightly cooked, since it reduces greatly in volume when cooked. Spinach contains both iron and calcium, but the absorption of these minerals by the human body is inhibited by the oxalic acid also found in spinach.

Serves 4 / Preparation time: 30 minutes, plus rising / Cooking time: 25 minutes / Oven temperature: 240°C (475°F), Gas Mark 9

Potato Dough Calzone

Potato dough:

25 g (1 oz) fresh yeast

350 ml (12 fl oz) lukewarm water

400 g (13 oz) strong plain flour, plus extra for
  working the dough

1 teaspoon salt

150 g (5 oz) cooked, sieved potato

butter, for greasing

Filling:

125 g (4 oz) lean cooked ham, cubed

250 g (8 oz) mozzarella cheese, cubed

250 g (8 oz) ricotta cheese

1 teaspoon chopped basil

2 eggs, beaten, plus extra for glazing

salt and pepper

1. Begin by making the dough. Blend the yeast with a little of the lukewarm water. Sieve the flour and salt into a large mixing bowl. Stir in the sieved potato. Make a well in the centre and pour in the yeast mixture and the remaining lukewarm water. Using your hand, and with a circular movement, gradually work the floury potato mixture into the liquid, working from the centre of the well outwards to make a sticky elastic dough.

2. Turn the dough on to a lightly floured surface and knead it well, adding more flour if necessary, until it is less sticky. Knead well for about 10 minutes, until the dough becomes smooth and elastic.

3. Sprinkle the base of the mixing bowl with flour. Return the dough to the bowl, cover with a cloth and leave the dough to rise until doubled in size – about 1 hour.

4. Meanwhile, mix all the filling ingredients together, adding salt and pepper to taste.

5. When the dough has risen, turn it on to a floured surface and divide into 8 pieces. Press each one out into a round, about 15 cm (6 inches) in diameter.

6. Divide the filling between the 8 rounds of dough. Moisten the edges of the rounds with a little water and fold each one over to form a semicircle, pinching the edges together well to seal them.

7. Brush the calzone with a little beaten egg. Place on a greased baking sheet and bake at the top of a preheated oven, 240°C (475°F), Gas Mark 9, for about 25 minutes, until well risen and golden brown.

FOOD FACT Calzone are small pizza turnovers. These ones can be fried instead of baked in the oven. Fried calzone are softer and lighter than the baked variety as they do not form a crust. To fry calzone, omit the egg glazing and fry them in hot, deep oil for about 4–5 minutes on each side. Drain well on kitchen paper and serve immediately.

Spanish Tortilla

150 ml (¼ pint) extra virgin olive oil
750 g (1½ lb) potatoes, thinly sliced
1 large onion, sliced
1 red pepper, deseeded and sliced
1 green pepper, deseeded and sliced
5 large eggs, beaten
salt and pepper

This is an authentic Spanish tortilla, which is traditionally made with just eggs, potatoes, onions and salt and pepper and cooked in a large amount of olive oil. This version contains sliced red and green peppers for extra colour and flavour.

1. Heat all but 2 tablespoons of the oil in a 20 cm (8 inch) nonstick frying pan. Add the potato slices, onion and red and green peppers and cook, stirring frequently, for 15 minutes, until all the vegetables are golden and tender.
2. Stir the potato mixture into a bowl containing the beaten eggs and season generously with salt and pepper. Set aside for 15 minutes. Clean the frying pan.
3. Heat the remaining oil in the clean pan and tip in the tortilla mixture. Cook over a low heat for 10 minutes, until almost cooked through. Carefully slide the tortilla on to a large plate. Invert another plate over the tortilla and turn the plates upside down so that you can slide the tortilla back into the frying pan, cooked side uppermost.
4. Return the pan to the heat and cook for a further 5 minutes, or until the tortilla is cooked on both sides. Allow to cool then serve the tortilla at room temperature, cut into wedges.

Malaysian Beef and Potato Curry

2 tablespoons groundnut oil

5 shallots, chopped

2 garlic cloves, crushed

5 cm (2 inch) piece of fresh root ginger, grated

2 tablespoons hot curry powder

1 teaspoon ground cinnamon

1 teaspoon ground cumin

1 teaspoon ground coriander

¼ teaspoon ground cardamom

4 curry leaves

1 star anise

4 cloves

375 g (12 oz) sirloin steak, cut into 1 cm
(½ inch) strips

300 g (10 oz) potatoes, peeled and cut into
medium-sized chunks

2 large fresh red chillies, deseeded and
finely chopped

½ teaspoon salt

300 ml (½ pint) coconut milk

juice of 1 lime

1 teaspoon soft brown sugar

plain boiled rice, to serve

1. Heat the oil in a saucepan, add the shallots, garlic and ginger and fry over a gentle heat, stirring frequently, for 5 minutes, or until softened. Add the curry powder, ground cinnamon, cumin, coriander and cardamom, the curry leaves, star anise and cloves, and fry for a further 1 minute.
2. Add the strips of beef and stir well to coat in the spice mixture. Add the potatoes, chillies, salt and coconut milk. Stir well to combine, bring to the boil, then lower the heat. Cover the pan and simmer gently, stirring occasionally, for 40 minutes, until the beef is tender and the potatoes are cooked.
3. Stir in the lime juice and sugar and cook, uncovered, for a further 2 minutes. Taste and adjust the seasoning, if necessary, then serve the curry hot, with plain rice.

Index